The King and I

Shakespeare

Shakespeare Now!
Series edited by Ewan Fernie and Simon Palfrey

The King and I

Philippa Kelly

continuum

'In *The King and I*, Philippa Kelly gives us an original and very personal response to a play she obviously loves and knows intimately. Remarkably, she is able to use the play as a prism through which to contemplate her life journey and to construct a commentary on modern Australia – refreshing and insightful.'

John Bell, AO, OBE

'In *The King and I*, Philippa Kelly has done a rare thing: she has written an original and deeply personal book about a Shakespearean tragedy that has been the object of exhausting and seemingly exhaustive critical attention. By bringing her life experience to bear on *King Lear*, by opening herself so completely and undefensively to its words and characters, Kelly illuminates the play's enduring power and freshness. At once a touching autobiographical memoir and a reflection on Australian history and culture, *The King and I* is a meditation on the contemporary relevance of Shakespeare's most searing tragedy.'

**Stephen Greenblatt, Author of *Will in the World:
How Shakespeare Became Shakespeare***

'A strikingly original meditation on *King Lear* and Australian life, in which both the play and the culture are illuminated.'

Barry Oakley, Australian novelist and playwright

'For teachers who agonise over how to make Shakespeare "relevant", this is a luminously inspiring book. Kelly has packaged her wisdom and insights in an absolute page-turner about a girl growing to be adult and citizen, her mates from *Lear* always at her side. She shows how *Lear* can transform lives. What a gem!'

Robert Hodge, *Myths of Oz* and *Darkside of the Dream*

Continuum International Publishing Group

The Tower Building
11 York Road
London SE1 7NX

80 Maiden Lane
Suite 704
New York, NY 10038

www.continuumbooks.com

British Library Cataloguing-in-Publication Data
A catalogue record for this book is available from the British Library.

ISBN: 978-1-4411-7868-8 (hardback)
      978-1-4411-1164-7 (paperback)

Library of Congress Cataloging-in-Publication Data
Kelly, Philippa.
The King and I / Philippa Kelly.
   p. cm. – (Shakespeare now!)
Includes bibliographical references and index.
ISBN 978-1-4411-7868-8 – ISBN 978-1-4411-1164-7 (pbk.)
1. Shakespeare, William, 1564–1616. King Lear. 2. Lear, King (Legendary character),
in literature. 3. National characteristics, Australian, in literature. 4. Kelly, Philippa. I. Title.

PR2819.K376 2010
822.33–dc22

                                                                2010029089

Typeset by Newgen Imaging Systems Pvt Ltd, Chennai, India
Printed and bound in India by Replika Press Pvt Ltd

To Peter Bailey

Human Rights advocate, extraordinary reader,
dearest of friends

Contents

General Editors' Preface to the Second-Wave of the Series

We begin with the passions of the critic as they are forged and explored in Shakespeare. These books speak directly from that fundamental experience of losing and remaking yourself in art. This does not imply, necessarily, a lonely existentialism; the story of a self is always bound up in other stories, shared tales of nations or faiths or of families large and small. But such stories are also always singular, irreducible to the generalities by which they are typically explained. Here, then, is where literary experience stops pretending to institutionalized objectivity, and starts to tell its own story.

Shakespeare Now! is a rallying cry, above all for aesthetic immediacy. It favours a model of aesthetic knowledge as *encounter*, where the encounter brings its own, often surprising contextualizing imperatives. Implicit in this is the premise that art is as much a subject as an object, less like aggregated facts and more like a fascinating person or persons. And encountering the plays as such is unavoidably personal.

Much recent scholarship has been devoted to Shakespeare *then* – to producing more information about the presumed moment of their inception. But this moment of inception is in truth happening over and over, again and again, anywhere that Shakespeare is being experienced anew or freshly. For the fact is that he remains, by a country mile, the most important *contemporary* writer – the most performed and read, the most written about, but also the most remembered. But it is not a question merely of Shakespeare in the present, as though his vitality is best measured by his passing relevance to great events. It is about his works' abiding *presence*.

In some ways criticism needs to get younger – to recover the freshness of aesthetic experience, and so in part better to remember why any of us should care. We need a new directness, written responses to the plays which attest to the life we find in them and the life they find in us.

Ewan Fernie and Simon Palfrey

General Editors' Preface

Shakespeare Now! represents a new form for new approaches. Whereas academic writing is far too often ascendant and detached, attesting all too clearly to years of specialist training, *Shakespeare Now!* offers a series of intellectual adventure stories: animate with fresh and often exposed thinking, with ideas still heating in the mind.

This series of 'minigraphs' will thus help to bridge two yawning gaps in current public discourse. First, the gap between scholarly thinking and a public audience: the assumption of academics that they cannot speak to anyone but their peers unless they hopelessly dumb-down their work. Second, the gap between public audience and scholarly thinking: the assumption of regular playgoers, readers or indeed actors that academics write about the plays at a level of abstraction or specialization that they cannot hope to understand.

But accessibility should not be mistaken for comfort or predictability. Impatience with scholarly obfuscation is usually accompanied by a basic impatience with anything but (supposed) common sense. What this effectively means is a distrust of really thinking, and a disdain for anything that might unsettle conventional assumptions, particularly through crossing or redrafting formal, political or theoretical boundaries. We encourage such adventure, and base our claim to a broad audience upon it.

Here, then, is where our series is innovative: no compromising of the sorts of things that can be thought; a commitment to publishing powerful cutting-edge scholarship; *but* a conviction that these things are essentially communicable, that we can find a language that is enterprising, individual and shareable.

To achieve this we need a form that can capture the genuine challenge and vigour of thinking. Shakespeare is intellectually exciting, and so too are the ideas and debates that thinking about his work can provoke. But published scholarship often fails to communicate much of this. It is difficult to sustain excitement over the 80–120,000 words customary for a monograph: difficult enough for the writer, and perhaps even more so for the reader. Scholarly articles have likewise become a highly formalized mode not only of publication, but also of intellectual production. The brief length of articles means that a concept can be outlined, but its implications or application can rarely be tested in detail. The decline of sustained, exploratory attention to the singularity of a play's language, occasion or movement is one of the unfortunate results. Often 'the play' is somehow assumed, a known and given thing that is not really worth exploring. So we spend our time pursuing collateral contexts: criticism becomes a belated, historicizing footnote.

Important things have got lost. Above all, any vivid sense as to why we are bothered with these things in the first place. Why read? Why go to plays? Why are they important? How does any pleasure they give relate to any of the things we labour to say about them? In many ways, literary criticism has forgotten affective and political immediacy. It has assumed a shared experience of the plays and then averted the gaze from any such experience, or any testing of it. We want a more ductile and sensitive mode of production; one that has more chance of capturing what people are really thinking and reading about, rather than what the pre-empting imperatives of journal or respectable monograph tend to encourage.

Furthermore, there is a vast world of intellectual possibility – from the past and present – that mainstream Shakespeare criticism has all but ignored. In recent years there has been a move away from 'theory' in literary studies: an aversion to its obscure jargon and complacent self-regard; a sense that its tricks were too easily rehearsed and that the whole game has become one of diminishing returns. This has further encouraged a retreat into the supposed safety of historicism. Of course the best such work is stimulating, revelatory and indispensable. But too often there is little trace of any struggle; little sense that the writer is coming at the subject afresh, searching for the most appropriate language or method. Alternatively, the prose is so laboured that all trace of an urgent story is quite lost.

We want to open up the sorts of thinking – and thinkers – that might help us get at what Shakespeare is doing or why Shakespeare matters. This might include psychology, cognitive science, theology, linguistics, phenomenology, metaphysics, ecology, history, political theory; it can mean other art forms such as music, sculpture, painting, dance; it can mean the critical writing itself becomes a creative act.

In sum, we want the minigraphs to recover what the Renaissance 'essay' form was originally meant to embody. It meant an 'assay' – a trial or a test of something; putting something to the proof; and doing so in a form that is not closed-off and that cannot be reduced to a system. We want to communicate intellectual activity at its most alive: when it is still exciting to the one doing it; when it is questing and open, just as Shakespeare is. Literary criticism – that is, really thinking about words in action, plays as action – can start making a much more creative and vigorous contribution to contemporary intellectual *life*.

Simon Palfrey and Ewan Fernie

Acknowledgements

My first thanks go to Simon Palfrey and Ewan Fernie, who understood what I was trying to do before I understood it myself. Their enormous intelligence, erudition, care and creativity have inspired me throughout this journey with Lear. (I could never have made the journey without them.) To Anna Fleming and Continuum Press, thank you for your belief in this book.

To my other dedicated readers and commentators I also give untold thanks: Ronald Bedford, Chandran Kukathas, R. S. White, Larry Smith, Derek Cohen and Paul Dresher, all of whom have given astute and bountiful comments.

No matter how interesting an octogenarian man, years of wrestling with him can be wearing. How fortunate I have been to have women in my life who have tempered this experience. Sharyn Charnas, Lisa Hubbell, Deborah O'Grady, Heather Smith, Pauline Kerr, Mary Duryee, Helen Meyer, Marcy Wong, Naomie Kremer, Pauline Vedelago, Susie Medak, Liz Lutz, Heller Rathbone, Martha Bielawski, Myriam Misrach, Julie Woodward, Jenny Lizzio, Sara M., Margit Roos Collins and Jan Bowman – you have all given precious insights into family, friendship, loyalty.

To Clive Yeabsley, who died in 2003, I owe my lifelong fascination with King Lear, and to Stephen Greenblatt I owe the inspiration for rethinking literature's place in my life. Thanks to John Bell and to my students from ADFA, especially Clare Swiderski and Chelsea McCubbery. Thanks to the women of Mullawah, and to Michael Rimmer, who provided me with memories of Clive Yeabsley and a digitized copy of my grandfather's interview from 1974. James Keller, Melissa Lane, John Argue, Charles Kremer, Megan Barton, Natasha Beery and P. L. Scott contributed some marvellous thoughts.

The California Shakespeare Theater has afforded me years of wonderful hands-on experience in the theatre, and the University of New South Wales provided institutional support

The loving friendship and great wisdom of my sister, Patience Kelly, runs deeply beneath these pages. My beloved son Cole, my husband Paul and my brothers, Simon, John and Benedict Kelly, are also integral to my sense of who I am. And my dear mother and father, I love you very much, and owe you more than I can say.

All references to *King Lear* are from the Folio edition, *The Norton Shakespeare*, eds. Greenblatt et al. (New York: Norton, 1997).

Introduction

'Speak what we feel, not what, we ought to say.'

For me, *King Lear* is alive. It has long held intensely personal meaning, with its searing portrayal of the wounds that can be opened by words. But as I have grown older, I have also come to see in the play a significance beyond the personal – reflecting my experience of Australian identity and culture. Of course this sense of Australianness isn't a single or a static thing, any more than the play is. Still less is it something finally understood or firmly in the past. Hence the mental journeying that is in this book.

Both Australia and *King Lear* are forces that I am always catching up with. Neither is for me a simple, comfortable fit. Like many Australians, I was born elsewhere and so I am 'of' Australia and yet removed from it, first a childhood immigrant, many years later an adult emigrant. In its own way, *King Lear* is a no less complicated kind of home. Who can dwell for long or at peace in Shakespeare's turbulent, even repellent world? But can anyone who has deeply experienced the force of that world ever resist returning, even if only in the imagination?

Australia and *King Lear* have become entwined in my reflections as a kind of furniture for the mind, by means of which I've come to orient myself and my memory, my feeling of continuity, my sense of possibility. This book is, necessarily, more than an individual story: it is also my take on a tale of national identity, of a country's wit, crises, and, at times, shame.

The King and I interweaves my personal experiences with some of the public discourses that have been cultivated by Australians: political ruptures, institutional oddities, cultural folklore, humorous skits, and performances both conservative and iconoclastic, all of which have drawn in vital ways upon *King Lear*. My aim is not merely to paint a Lear-coloured landscape of Australian history, nor even to refashion the gold-fringed land down under as a blasted heath. I want to reveal aspects of the past that we might be surprised to find, or that we might too casually have forgotten. These things are past but not gone; the traces linger. In this book, *King Lear* is my dramatic touchstone, helping me to call up voices from the past (including its own), all of them asking to be heard and spoken and heard once again.

* * *

Some people may recall a scene, or a moment, or a few lines, from *King Lear* that have hung on in their minds. An image or a group of words can stimulate thoughts and ideas even seemingly far removed from the experience of the play itself, and *King Lear* is part of the fabric – dusty, long-undisturbed – laid down during the educational years of many Australians.[1] This book explores the diverse places in our national sensibility into which the play has filtered. It may affect some people in the moment of watching or reading, yielding meaning for the time it takes to crank out an essay, and remaining, perhaps, as barely a wisp of memory. But for others, whether it be due to the way the play is taught or their state of mind when they encounter it, Shakespeare's magnificent, tortured landscape will provide an active and enduring role in their understanding of themselves in the world. This is the manner in which I came to *King Lear*, or, indeed, it came to me.

If asked to give a nutshell view of what it is 'about', the play would seem most clearly to revolve around a king. But more deeply it concerns fathers and children, great, imperfect love, misplaced authority and missed connections. It begins with a father who believes he can command love from his daughters in return for the land he is now willing to disburse, since death will so soon take the land from him anyway. As a consequence of the love-test he imposes on his daughters, all three of them make breaks with his authority, and these breaks fire the engine of dramatic impact in the play.

It is this volatile relationship between fathers, children and authority that finds a palpable connection with Australia's recent history. If you walk around the oldest area of Sydney, The Rocks, you will see the marks of paternal authority as it was inscribed upon the land: the two hundred and thirty year-old buildings erected in the scorching sun block-by-block by those ancestors who were hardy enough to survive the six-month transportation from England (including Ann Martin, my maternal grandmother nine generations removed, sent out for the crime of stealing three silk handkerchiefs). Australia's immigrants brought with them the memories of far-off fathers: the English ones who'd used the First Fleet to disburden themselves of their social rejects; and then later, in the twentieth century, the Asians and Europeans whose offspring came willingly to seek prosperity. Leaving behind their fathers to 'settle' this new land, they brushed aside the bones of the forgotten fathers to whom the land belonged.

These immigrants – the first of them unwillingly deposited in a place they saw as adversarial, and the latter who laboured at menial jobs to carve a place in their midst – had not much time for brooding. In general, Australians are still reluctant (publicly, at least) to use an extensive emotional vocabulary to address deep psychic wounds such as those that are played out in the Lear family. We often like to see ourselves as easy-going, unfussy people with a rugged sensibility and a ready wit. But this doesn't mean that we are thoroughly uncomplicated; and *The King and I* aims to expose some of our cultural complexities. On occasion we might be rulers, insisting on the rights of heredity and precedent. At others we are dependents, struggling to define our own voices. In the complex layout of our history, we are fathers, we are children, servants, Fools and kings. And sometimes we are blind, ignoring those whose wounds we have inflicted.

In *The King and I*, Australians will sometimes be referred to as 'they', sometimes 'we'. This is perhaps the language of an expatriate who is striving both to analyse and to express a sense of identity. The book will bring into focus many parts of my history and sensibility as an Australian. The shadow of *King Lear*, recreated in a new reign afresh, stretches from England's Commonwealth across our beaches and our red-dirt land. We are still yoked as children to the 'mother country', and *King Lear* can embody part of that story. For Americans, Australian culture resonates because of the many historical analogues we share. There is the role of the wilderness and the pioneers who tame it; the sense of individual autonomy and possibility; the establishment of cultural identity to be reconciled with the encroachment on indigenous peoples; and the figure of the outlaw striking out against authority's injustices. These are largely the narratives of people creating culture and society where no laws were believed to have existed: fundamental to them is the idea of authority, and of its rupture. To illuminate and question who and where we are now, and to shed fresh light on places we've been: this is the purpose of my journey with the King.

Chapter 1
Fathers and Mothers

As the years have gone on and we have spread out over the world, I have come to recognize how deeply I am a part of my original family. Now, we meet infrequently as a group on a sunny verandah in Brisbane or Sydney, our parents sitting in squatters' chairs, their old legs supported by the long wooden beams, we five 'kids' carrying on the jokes and conversation around and above them. These days we approve of each other after all those early years of anxious influence, and we sit watching our kids benignly as they play hide and seek and get stuck in drains as we used to. More than thirty-five years ago, we were five white-blonde kids who rode our bicycles around the verandah or the town. The older boys excelled in sports and public speaking and collected cows' skulls as museum exhibits that cost 2 cents a look. I had my dolls and my books, the terrors of Catholicism and Mortal Sin, my love of my younger sister's companionship and my monstrous reign over her because I was 3 years older and very wise. I was ripe for *King Lear*. I only had to discover it.

In this chapter I have chosen to focus on the time when I first encountered the play as a teenager in the 1970s. It might seem slightly peculiar that a book about an old king will begin so strongly with my mother's presence. My mother is integral to my sense of myself, and her strength and vision were what I came to believe and to trust in. She is also integral to the inside place – the place of unworthiness, where ideals hit the quicksand, a place where my father struggled each day, deeply loving his family but insisting that we conform to his image of himself and the world and of who he felt his children ought to be. My mother saw this place of unworthiness as well, but she preferred its disquieting images to remain deeply interred.

King Lear, Queensland, 1976

In 1967 our family emigrated from England to Australia under the 'Assisted Passage' programme. This was part of the blinkered White Australia policy prevailing from the time of Australia's Federation in 1901 until 1973, when the left-wing Whitlam Government signed off on its termination.[2] The Assisted Passage programme allowed Britons to fly to Australia for 10 pounds apiece – and, as my mother was eight-and-a-half months pregnant with my youngest brother, we didn't even have to pay for him.

About a year after we arrived in Australia our family settled in a town called Oakey, two and a half hours' drive west of Brisbane, Queensland's sprawling, dusty capital. The move to Oakey was made on a whim because my father hated Brisbane, where we'd first landed and started to build our lives. My mother, who was born in Australia and had travelled to England as a 26-year-old, returning 10 years later with an English husband and four children (almost five), had been evacuated to Oakey as a child during the Second World War. She wanted to see again the convent where she and her sisters had lived for 3 years without their parents. Visiting Oakey in the late 1960s, my parents liked the look of the town, and they also saw that an army base was being built, which would require temporary accommodation to be made available in the town. So, with no experience at all in the hospitality industry, they borrowed some money from my grandparents, and my Dad built a small country motel. He would work all week in Brisbane selling insurance, and, on the weekends, make the 2-hour drive to Oakey to work as a labourer with his building team for the year it took to complete the motel. My Dad had been a paratrooper before he left his teens, a farmer; a Nuffield Scholar who travelled to America on an agricultural scholarship, an insurance broker. Now, at the age of forty-five, he had a new trade in a new land. He was always meant to be king of his own patch, and Kelly's Motel suited him well.

A man of considerable charisma, my Dad was also, in his middle age, strained with the responsibility of providing for a large family. He would get up at first light to work with the handwritten accounts and the heavy wooden cash box and to deliver the breakfasts, sliding them into little hatches outside each motel room by 7 a.m. regardless of the time requested. By 7.30 or 8 he would heavily deposit a bucket of cleaning equipment outside the door of guest room number 1, the signal that Dad was ready to get on with his day and so should the occupants be as well.

Stitched into my memory are the hot, still mornings broken by the shrieking of koalas high up in the gum trees; the motel towels, fading stiffly in the sun; the little white nets hung over bowls of sugar or swampy butter. Almost all of our garbage (including next door's strangled rooster, which Dad discreetly disposed of because it woke up our motel guests) would go into the incinerator out the back of the house, in the days before anyone thought of legislating against damage to the environment. They were the days before people thought much about legislating against inequity of any kind, in fact. I remember that an accident happened early one morning outside the motel, and my mother asked our next-door neighbour whether anyone had been hurt. 'No,' was the reply. 'Only an Aboriginal.'

My mother has herself delivered many distinctive (though less dreadful) commentaries over the years. 'A dear, dear man, and he's ageing beautifully'; 'Audrey's doing marvellously. Almost too marvellously, in fact. Dad's sick of her telling him how good she feels not to have a drink.' 'There was a group of large women with loud voices and small, impoverished-looking husbands.' My mother has, to this day, a mind both free and serrated with keen judgment, with an imagination that soars well beyond the lines of her natural restraint.

Being a Catholic, my mother had spent the first 10 years of her marriage either pregnant or recovering from childbirth. After we moved to Oakey, however, she was compelled for financial reasons to practise her profession as a pharmacist, despite my father's preference that she be available at home. During various holiday periods she worked for weeks at a stretch as a locum, or visiting practitioner, in pharmacies around Oakey, and also in Toowoomba, a small city 20 miles away from where we lived. She still cooked all of the breakfasts each morning for the motel, and often, to meet the requirements for mothers of the swimming team, put in the oven with the crisping bacon a cake that we kids hid at the back of the trestle table adjacent to the pool. She shot off to the pharmacy each day with a mixture of gratefulness and guilt.

She had three alternating temporary jobs, the most regular of which was at the Bailey Henderson, the pharmacy department of a mental hospital in Toowoomba. The Bailey Henderson had been built in the 1890s, one of the first Australian institutions of its kind, since mental-health issues before that time had been dealt with on a case-by-case basis. The hospital was based on the structure of the Hospital of St Mary of Bethlehem (Bedlam) near London, itself first built in the thirteenth century and redesigned in the nineteenth century so that male and female wards were kept separate from each other. While there was a history of heavy custodial care at the Bailey, the manacled control of violent patients was beginning to change in the 1970s, when medications took the place of physical restraints.

Each day when Mum got home from the Bailey, there was dinner to cook for seven, homework to be supervised, and the kitchen to be cleaned and prepared for next morning's breakfasts. (I remember how fraught she would get when one of us went into the kitchen for an unscheduled snack. 'It's almost more than I can bear. Oh hell.') In the evenings after all this was done, she would fall onto the bed beside my youngest brother, Ben, while he was going off to sleep. She would ask him what he'd done at playgroup that day and he'd tell her that he'd bashed up the girls in the dollies' corner or he'd put the kittens down the toilet but got them out again. My mother would sigh groggily, 'That's lovely, darling . . . Precious lamb.'

In the days of my mother's locum shifts at the Bailey, people could be put in mental hospitals for all kinds of things that are unthinkable now. Children born with hideous deformities were often quietly shipped out there, where they stayed until they died. Many schizophrenics were at the Bailey for the whole of their adult lives, and my mother had the kind of personality that was very gentle with the peculiarities of strangers. (It was for her family that she reserved her substantial stores of on-the-spot correction.) She felt particularly for the trans-sexuals, who ended up at the Bailey during their hormone treatments, tucked away with their disgraceful hopes in a mental hospital.

In the long summer holidays she would occasionally let me come with her to the Bailey for the day because I liked to be close to her and to read. She liked to read, too, and one quiet summer out there she read the whole of *War and Peace.* I would sit to the side of the dispensary with a bag of sweets, reading Nancy Drew or Enid Blyton and absorbing the comforting awareness of my mother dispensing pills and calm advice. 'Take it with a cup of tea. That's always nice.' 'Doctor wants you to try this for a few weeks. It'll give you a marvelous lift.' By law, all of her interactions with the patients had to take place through a small window in the dispensary, with a guard in constant attendance jangling his keys. But even in these circumstances my mother's warmth and good sense brought consola-tion, and I remember the sound of her shockproof voice greeting the muffled sounds of confusion and despair. The man who spent his days, summer and winter, wrapped in a greatcoat covered with medals; the transsexuals in the middle of their transformations; the women who'd been left at the Bailey because no one could procure a future for them after late-teen nervous breakdowns – all of these people came to see my mother. For a woman who has cleaved all her life to the contours of propriety, she was remarkably able to treat each situation as something completely normal, with the empathy that has always been her spontaneous gift.

The patients at the Bailey, huddled together in a liminal universe, and the child in the corner of the dispensary who didn't understand this universe but felt its effects – the coldness, the voices dulled by brutal medications, the smell of musty cooked pumpkin, the sense of vacancy . . . It was a place I'd have been terrified to be in without my mother. Now, all these years later, I can see that truths were hidden at the Bailey, or perhaps they were exposed. The truth about the human mind, which is not always able to coordinate rational perception with fears and imaginings; the truth that your sexual organs need not dictate your real gender; the truth that an unbalanced face doesn't spell mental disproportion; the truth that 'normal' is just a word we throw around. One day two patients were squabbling outside the dining hall as my mother walked past, and one said to the other, 'You're mad'.

The bias against age, against nature, against madness; people shivering together, the rejects of the earth. It was in 1976, some years into my mother's sojourns at the Bailey, that I first experienced another place of lost identity, another place of emotion played out in a largely uncaring universe. An old, confused king, stripped of all his power, clinging to the memory of what he never was except in name and seeming power. The Bedlam beggar who is no less than any man, and far more than what he appears to be. The Fool who speaks truths that no one wants to hear. A group of people at the edge of the world, begging the dreadful question of what it means to be a person and what it takes to be seen, fully, as a human. This was the world of *King Lear*, introduced to my tenth grade class by a dynamic high-school teacher, Clive Yeabsley, who provoked in me a fascination with the play that would last for all of my life to date. I remember asking Clive (or Mr. Yeabsley, as we knew him then) what the word 'Bedlam' meant. He said, 'It was the name for Bethlehem, you know, places for the homeless and mentally ill – a bit like the place in Toowoomba.' He had no idea that my mother worked there nor how well I knew it.

The 1960s in Australia had seen an overhaul of the secondary education system in Queensland. Public examinations were abolished, and, for a brief period in the 1970s, teachers had considerable flexibility in choosing the materials they taught, as well as in the way they interpreted their materials. *King Lear* was chosen by Mr. Yeabsley for study in a syllabus that included James Joyce's *Portrait of the Artist as a Young Man,* the poetry of Gerald Manley Hopkins, and D. H. Lawrence's *Sons and Lovers.* For two months, twice a week (on Tuesdays and Fridays), we spent an hour or sometimes two on *King Lear*, beginning each class with a segment from a televised version of the play, or, occasionally, acting out scenes from the play ourselves.

My first memory of the play is the first time we watched it on screen – the love-test that Lear engineers in the play's opening scene. I was a kid who was quite secluded from life, young for my class and daunted by my older brothers' popularity. So I lived largely in the world of my imagination with my books and the terrors of the Catholic Church. I was enormously connected to my parents, a tricky allegiance because in those days Dad was warm and very loving and profoundly unavailable. I feared causing him anger, even more humiliation. The time I did bring it on, clearly and indisputably, by being the subject of a letter saying I was Not Living Up to Potential, Dad berated me for weeks about the special horror for an Englishman of receiving such a letter via Her Majesty's Service (the post).

For a person so thoroughly enmeshed within her family, it was shocking to witness Cordelia's rebuke that first day in the English class, on BBC TV as imported to an Australian classroom. Yet I also understood that in the face of her father's clawing determination to have her all to himself, Cordelia makes a choice to effect this violent separation. I understood this then, and yet not deeply nor clearly enough to imagine what it could mean for myself or for any girl.

All through my life, until recent years, I have been unwilling to separate from various kinds of obligation and authority. In new situations I have usually been comforted by nostalgia (an idealized home that has no room for darkness),[3] and I have often let other people make decisions for me and then wriggled around to find a comfortable situation, not always without complaint. Over many years I learned to become as flexible as a contortionist; but I have also at times surprised other people with a passive resistance that they did not anticipate. I have sometimes suffered, and caused disquiet, for not being willing to name my own strength and find my own place to exercise it freely.

In the days of Mr. Yeabsley's class, the world was still unfocused because it existed so fully in my imagination, with my books and my fears and my horrible church and the old, cross nuns at the Mass with their wimpled heads itching in the heat. Mr. Yeabsley was a force from another world. For a start, he lived in Toowoomba, a glamorous figure who commuted from the metropolis each day to enlighten us in Oakey. But much more importantly, he asked us questions about the meaning of love; about the expression of love in public settings; about being asked to trade declarations of loyalty in return for material benefit; and about the pressure exerted in any relationship when the balance of power is wildly uneven. 'A relationship should always be conducted on the basis of the person who wants least,' he said, 'because that person has more power'. But who wants least in the play's first scene: the old king who craves love, or the daughters whose wants are shaped in relationship to him?

In *King Lear*'s first scene, the Lear family's past is alluded to, but we have to conjure its shape and complexion for ourselves. The old man, Lear, has had, in abundance, all that the world can offer. What he most wants now is for his beloved youngest daughter to declare – publicly, so he can believe it – that she loves him. He offers her the greatest measure he possesses (the kingdom of England, the finest slice), and he expects to become a dependent, or even a babe again, in the warmth of her 'kind nursery' (1.1.122). He is utterly unprepared for her rebuke, 'Nothing, my lord' (1.1.85). 'Speak again,' he says (1.1.88), to which she elaborates, 'I love your majesty / According to my bond, no more nor less' (1.1.90–1). There it is: a series of negatives, words that baldly declare through the limits of language the limits of love. Much has been written on the topic of Cordelia's expression of a love that transcends the limits of language: but,

Mr. Yeabsley pointed out to us, isn't she just being difficult? Can't she *see* what he is really asking for?

In the face of Cordelia's rebuke, the king's whole self is exposed. He is both literally and metaphorically 'dis-graced',[4] since his response to Cordelia prompts him to end his regency by crudely chopping his kingdom down the middle and handing it out to his other two daughters. He is emotionally naked and starving. And in the course of the next several scenes he becomes *physically* naked, needy, left out in the cold – until, at his lowest ebb, he is embraced by his youngest daughter, who returns chastened from France to give him the very solace he had wanted in the first place. It might seem implausible to think of young teens grasping all of this – and yet, in a sense, who better than teens to do so, since we could imagine how grossly embarrassing it would be to be asked by our fathers in the town hall to declare, in front of all the other parents, how much we loved them? And who better than teens to understand Lear himself, who begins the play in his own extended childhood, insisting on making '[his] daughters [his] mothers' (1.4.137–8)?

Although Lear's initial command is for love to be served up to him, in the course of the play he learns that in the truest kind of love we are indeed servants to each other, and that an act of love is a service of the heart.[5] In 1.4 the banished Kent couples service with love in the beautiful lines that take him back into Lear's company disguised as the servant Caius: 'If thou canst serve where thou does stand condemn'd, / So it may come, thy master, whom thou lovest, / Shall find thee full of labours' (1.4. 5–7). Lear, who had thought of love as pay-on-demand, makes a terrible journey (with his loyal band of servants and fellow rejects) in which he discovers the true nature and expression of love. He is finally able to express its shared humility: 'When thou dost ask my blessing, I'll kneel down, / And ask of thee forgiveness' (5.3.10–11). His passage towards this perception is shadowed by that of his old friend the Earl of Gloucester, who laments that his 'dear son Edgar' has been the food of his wrath, and, through his suffering, learns the paradoxical capacity to 'see thee in my touch' (4.1.23–4). In my years of travelling through time and place since the days of Oakey, I have seen that the problem of blindness is not unique to Lear and Gloucester. How many people (including myself) have I heard lamenting, 'He just doesn't meet my needs!' 'She doesn't understand me!' The true source and spring of love is a mutual capacity to serve and to receive. The place where we learn to experience this – and to *not* see it – is in our families, those places of intense, chaotic, misdirected love. We teenagers all had families, and we were just starting to understand the mysteries of things that had always been 'done' but yet not talked about within our families' special codes. It is families that first expose their children to such mysteries, and to the limitless possibilities for mis-speaking our intentions and mis-hearing what we ought to understand.

Becoming a Woman

King Lear gives its women very few lines, as well as narrow parameters for self-expression.[6] It is a 'corseting' of sorts. There is Cordelia, whose plain speaking costs her the most verdant part of her father's kingdom. Some girls might identify with her capacity for bluntness; but for many she will become a distant paragon, a speaker of plain truth who comes back to save her father and is slaughtered. Then there are Regan and Goneril, who ultimately destroy each other with the power their father gives them. Is this depiction of womanly extremes Shakespeare's way of illustrating the 'proper' constraints of womanhood? Do women who speak too honestly lose all, while women who get hold of material power disrupt the 'natural' state of things? Order is eventually restored in this play, after all, only when all three women are killed off.

Although we talked extensively in class about the first scene and imagined the excruciating emotion of the love-test, the three daughters – who appear after the first scene primarily to illuminate their father's emotional journey – quickly became, in our imaginations, embodiments of animal imagery or of 'the bond' of true love. Our discussions excluded altogether Lear's shocking prayer for his eldest daughter's sterility (1.4.240) and his reference to the 'hell' of a woman's genitals: the 'sulphurous pit . . . burning, scalding, stench, consumption' (4.6.121–2).[7] This avoidance of the daughters' womanhood may have been an age-appropriate choice on Mr. Yeabsley's part. I still think, however, that without considering the expectations and limits placed on these characters as women, it is difficult to think of them as 'real'. Maybe it is not until you have experienced the complexity of life, the constraints of gender, the value of money and the cost of not having it, that Goneril and Regan can indeed become real.

In 1976, we girls were just growing into the subject of what 'makes' a woman, as we experimented to varying effect with wedge heels, green eye shadow and attitude. But in various parts of the world (and even of Australia) in the 1970s, women's selves and rights were being vigorously appraised. In 1972 Australian singer Helen Reddy, tired of fronting for male bands who would come to the microphone and tell her to wait out the back for them once the concert was over, made an international hit with *I am Woman* ('I am woman, hear me roar / In numbers too big to ignore').[8] And at the same time Australian feminist Germaine Greer published *The Female Eunuch*, a book that would remain for many years a trailblazer for feminists all over the world.[9] For Greer, suburban nuclear families devitalized women, turning them into compliant eunuchs. She saw women as repressed, cut off from their natural appetites, functioning within a realm of diminutive choices. Greer believed that from childhood, the women of her time were taught to make a virtue out of subjugation. If you turn these ideas on their heads, she argued, you can see how duped you've been by a society whose very structures of morality and etiquette and whose permissions for behaviour are structured for the benefit of men.[10]

Some of our mothers had heard of the fuss generated by *The Female Eunuch*; but they saw their countrywoman's vigorous arguments on behalf of their liberation as part of the silly far-off city nonsense that was talked about on the radio.[11] In 1976, many of us teenagers walked around humming the song 'Howzat' by a band called Sherbet, which topped the charts for four straight weeks, a dull tune that irritated me even then, although I found myself humming it nonetheless. *I've been looking at you, / Looking closely at the things you do / I didn't see it the way you wanted me to. / How, how, howzat? / You messed about / I caught you out, howzat? Now that I found where you're at / It's goodbye / Well howzat? / It's goodbye* . . . (trailing off on a long wail). This was of course a song – imprinted on a classic Aussie male cricketing template – about love and treachery, resulting in an inevitable 'You're out!' or 'goodbye'. Did we think about its connection to the play we were studying at school, in which a father acts like a lover who shouts a bitter 'goodbye'? Of course not. We helped vote five ABBA love songs into the top twenty-five for that year, knowing less about love than about whether we preferred the blonde or the brunette.

There was the boy in the class above mine, rumoured to have undergone *plastic surgery*, which offered intriguing images of a nose made of plastic. There was the girl my age who had sex on a school field trip and was labelled a slut until she left the twelfth grade. There was the man down the street who people said was a woman underneath. Such shared intolerances are the especial property of teenagers, whose task it is to complete *themselves* and to figure out who *they* are – which they typically do at the expense of understanding other people. In an elemental way, *King Lear* is all about the difficulties we were experiencing: about blindness, bad consequences and misinterpretations, played out in one of the world's most famously dysfunctional families. And, given the conspicuous absence of the mother (who was Mrs. Lear and when did she disappear?) the play was, in the mid-1970s, extraordinarily resonant with a culture where fathers ruled the roost. Some kids had fathers who swayed in church and smelled suspiciously of alcohol, which no one ever mentioned. If your cat produced a litter of kittens, it was your Dad who let you keep one or two and knocked the others on the head with a mallet.

It was acceptable for Dads to go down to the bowling club and get roaring drunk on Saturday afternoons while their wives caught up on chores; and on Sundays after Mass the men would congregate at the local pub while the wives sat outside with their children in hot, dusty cars.

We teenagers went to swimming carnivals and sat in the Cecil Café and ate chips, or lay on our beds and anticipated the next top ten on the nationwide teenage music show, *Countdown*. But we were, each one of us, in a state of becoming, and our fathers were also in transit: increasingly, they were less the repositories of wisdom than of flaws that embarrassingly shrank them. Parental assurances that tomorrow is a new day, parental admonitions that God sees everything, parental cries of you kids are killing me: by our teens, we were beginning to see past all this. We didn't require that things around us make sense, but we were starting to see that they didn't.

Lear in Double Vision

In 1975, the year before I was introduced to *King Lear*, an extraordinary event took place in Australian history. Australia's Prime Minister, Gough Whitlam, was sacked by the then Governor General, Sir John Kerr, who had been appointed as Whitlam's nominee and a trusted associate of his left-leaning Labor government. School stopped on 11 November 1975 while most of us crowded around the new television in the school hall and watched the analysis of the sacking – called The Dismissal – on the news. The public was baffled, as was the Prime Minister himself. Whitlam could not believe that his own chosen appointee would turn around and sack him.

Gough Whitlam's Labor government had been re-elected just a year previously, with one crucial weakness in its composition: because of what, in classic Australian style, was nominated 'the night of the long prawns', the government did not have a majority in the Senate.

The night of the long prawns referred to Whitlam's attempt to redress his Senate imbalance by replacing a retiring conservative senator with a left-wing nominee. The conservative senator in question had been lured away to an evening of beer and prawns which successfully forestalled his resignation, so that the conservatives continued their majority in the Senate and could crucially block the supply of financial bills planned to fund the government's extensive social reforms. This was the fatal weakness that gave Sir John Kerr his call to action.

On 11 November, 1975, Kerr stated to the nation that he had no possible option but to move to unblock the Senate: he handed Whitlam a letter of dismissal, requiring that his party face a general election in December of that year. Without approaching the Queen of England herself, Kerr used her authority in a manner that was unprecedented in Australia, and it was unprecedented even in England since the seventeenth century. This remains perhaps the single most significant day of politics in Australian history. Kerr instated Malcolm Fraser's conservative party as a caretaker government, and when the country went to the polls a month later in December 1975, citizens were driven by their fear of financial crisis so that the caretaker government was voted resoundingly into office.

The figure of Lear nudges at my memory as I look back at this scene and the characters involved. Whitlam's is the first image that comes to mind – this vastly tall politician with an equally towering wife, a charismatic pair who symbolized the rollicking free spirit of Australian leadership. Kerr would later say that Whitlam had had plenty of warning prior to the day of the Dismissal. But Whitlam – whose sense of decency was equalled by a naivety unusual in a politician – had supported Kerr in ways that signalled deep trust in the institution of government and in those empowered to participate in it. I recently interviewed a former senior government official who recalls that Kerr, before his appointment to the position of Governor General, asked him whether The Prime Minister would find it unseemly if he remarried just months after his first wife's death. The official put the question to Whitlam, who replied: 'A man's private business is a man's private business. It shouldn't affect how he fills his position in the government.' Who, having displayed again and again this sense of propriety, could imagine his own nominee deserting him? Only a man with too much hubris and too much decency to see. Only a Lear, perhaps, a man who would say, right after the Dismissal, 'Well may we say, God save the Queen, because nothing will save the Governor General.'[12] A man who, for many years after he lost the right to govern Australia, opened galleries and presided at official events, insisting that he was still every inch a king and treated as such by his admirers.

But there is another apprentice Lear here, lurking around the corner: a would-be Lear, someone who dressed in a top hat and coat tails in the middle of summer,[13] nursing great pride in his office. To help bring into focus this more shadowy Lear, let us recall the first scene of Shakespeare's play, by the end of which the old king's title has approximately the same meaning as it did for the queen of England in 1975, or, indeed, for Australia's Governor General. From the play's second scene onward Lear is a king in name only. The power of government belongs to Goneril and Regan, and to Edmund as granted by his father, the Earl of Gloucester. As part of a national audience, my family listened to Kerr's rather Lear-like Australia Day speech delivered two months after the Dismissal: 'As history unfolds, major events and problems occur, and the nation has to accommodate itself to the impact upon it of great forces. It has to make big decisions.'[14] For myself, when I read this speech now, I see how ironic is the gap that has emerged in history between Kerr's perception of his role and what that role *actually* was.

Although Kerr had been endorsed by Whitlam for the position of Governor General, it was commonly believed that he didn't feel sufficiently honoured or attended to within the engine of government. In sacking Whitlam's government and bringing down its leader, Kerr thought of himself as a man who changed the course of Australian history. Indeed, he *did* change the course of history – but once his massive, capricious action was completed he was in fact diminished. Seeing himself as an important engine of government, he misunderstood his principal function by confusing it with its glorious regal polish. He was the emissary of the Queen, herself the distantly luminous presence who dominated the women's magazines that lined the shelves of the local news agency. The Queen jetted into Australia on a royal plane so large that there were certain small cities she couldn't land in. 'The Queen', my mother announced one day, after an unheard-of spare ten minutes to bury her head in the *Women's Weekly* at the dentist's office, 'has the most beautiful skin': a note of wistful magic for Australian women who exposed their faces daily to the searing sun while hanging out the washing on the line. The Queen floated sublime above mundane activities, a protected, distant jewel in the eyes of her Australian people. The Queen had fresh toilet seats especially provided for her in every place she visited. She was, for Australians even back in 1975, a figurehead, a measure of social propriety and cultural protocol – a *symbol* of the exercise of government rather than an executive in herself. If the lofty figure of Whitlam evoked a Lear who thundered that he was every inch a king although his crown had been ripped away, Kerr made the fatal mistake of imagining that the crown he wore was real. It was never real. It was a papier mâché crown.

The story of the drama played out by these two figures illuminates the humanity of *King Lear's* folkloric first scene. This scene of misjudgment and inaccurate self-perception can repeat itself between people at home, or in the office, or in a community group, or in politics. And if the stage is grand enough, as it was for Whitlam and Kerr, the scene can rock the foundation of a country's government as well as its diplomatic relationships, creating an extraordinary situation in our history. Certainly a good solid reading of *King Lear*, or a serendipitous watching of a performance, would not have stopped either Whitlam or Kerr from doing what he did in 1975. But if we take the opportunity to contemplate this past event against the background of Shakespeare's play, basic human emotions – hubris, blindness, misaligned intentions – play out with a special meaning in our own cultural landscape. Whitlam's hubris was in his failure to properly judge the capabilities of the post of Governor General, as well as the personality of the man who occupied the post. Kerr's hubris was in confusing his self with his crown. In both, the failure to *see* converged in a disastrous misalliance.

As recently as 2010 the failure to see and hear, indeed, caused the downfall of Kevin Rudd, one of Australia's more visionary and ambitious Prime Ministers. Bureaucrats complained of being left for three years to rot in their offices preparing memos that would never be read and being told to prepare for meetings that would never take place. Rudd made decisions – snap decisions and plans for policies alleged to be improperly implemented – in consultation with a tiny pool of advisors. The bulk of Australia's governing machine was left to watch from the sidelines as initiatives like the economic recovery insulation plan went into gear,[15] leaving four people dead; as sweeping changes were made to the education sector to bring Australia closer to China; and as a resources tax was hastily put into motion against the grinding opposition of the mining industry. 'The grisly thud of kneecapped Rudd' was the summation given by one reporter:[16] after all of his ambitious plans for Australia, the story of Rudd's leadership became that of a man who ruled with calamitous arrogance. He was compelled by is own party to step down from his role as head of state. As he wept in front of the nation, Rudd served perhaps as a reminder that in a democratic country the Prime Minister sits at the head of an elected government, not atop a golden throne.

Chapter 2

Twenty Years Have Passed

1996: Unforeseen Beginnings

Leap forward with me 20 years, but not without viewing from the window of your imagination the young girl seduced by literature turning into a doctor of philosophy and teaching literature in various places, including the much-beloved tropical area of Far North Queensland. There I had my first teaching job. My office, with its desk and large laundry sink, was located in an old house that had been converted into B Block of the newly established Cairns Campus of James Cook University. Staff could bring their washing in and hang it on the rotary clothesline outside the 'admin' block. The hum of the cicadas, the students, young and barefoot, or middle-aged mothers who came to class in thongs and shorts. This was still my time of waiting – waiting to grow up, waiting for real life to begin, seeing myself as a girl although I passed the age of 30.

In 1996, I moved down south to become a tenured lecturer at the Australian Defence Force Academy, sent off by my North Queensland friends with a bag of marijuana and a fear of sniffing dogs. Completely different from the gentle, loose environment of Cairns, the Australian Defence Force Academy is located in Canberra, Australia's capital city, and caters to a select group of trainee officers. By the time they arrive in Canberra at the age of 17 ½ or 18, the cadets have chosen to place themselves for a period of at least ten years within one of the most structured forms of authority available to Australian youth. Some of them have done this for the sake of a 'free' education through the University of

New South Wales, which has an agreement with the Academy to provide the university component of the cadets' education: the return-of-service time for a four-year degree is six years (unless you can prove that you are unattractively disturbed). But many of these cadets are indeed vocationally driven: they want to serve Australia, and they look forward to their first posting. They also understand the military authority structure as something essential to action. For cadets at the Academy, weekdays routinely begin at 5 a.m. They have to get up and make their rooms impeccable for inspection, and then head out for drill, or for demanding group exercises. They breakfast at 7, return to dress in their uniforms and face inspection at 7.45, and are sitting in class by 8 a.m. After a full academic day, they face more exercises, drills and military classes in the evenings, as well as assignments to complete for their university classes.

Given that fatigue and time constraints are overriding concerns for these students, my immediate aim in putting together literature courses was to stave off their pressing urge to sleep. Students would often voluntarily stand up in my classes in order to stay awake, and I didn't take it personally. But by far my greater challenge was in understanding and making use of the structures of obedience that regulate the students' lives and duties at the Academy. They are getting paid to study within a stringent disciplinary environment, and the pressures imposed on them – especially since they are just fresh out of school – are considerable. If a senior training officer orders them to run 10 miles before breakfast, they cannot ask 'why'. If a full dress parade is called at 5 a.m., they cannot ask 'why'.[17] But 'why' is still a crucial guiding question for the internalization of authority; because it is by understanding authority's impacts and effects that one can learn to use it with intelligence and discretion. This kind of training can produce the very best kind of soldier – someone who follows orders in a split second in the most adverse conditions, but who has also learned to think. In other words, a model officer. Shakespeare's Hamlet (a scholar and not a soldier) gives an insight into the difficulty of achieving a balance between action and thought when he posits these faculties as essentially incompatible: if he acts, he relinquishes thought, and if he thinks, he is unable to act.

Some teachers go into the humanities at the Academy with the view that teaching should be revolutionary, a means by which to dare the students to disobey. I did not believe this – I thought (and still think) that rigorous structures of living and thinking can be successfully challenged if they are respected and understood. I hoped to stimulate, to challenge, to show the students that Shakespeare could provide an intriguing provocation to intellect and feeling. The very complexities of many of his metaphoric constructions, and of his rhyming and non-rhyming verse, exemplify the capacity to encapsulate multiple ideas within the borders of stylistic regularity.

I introduced to the literature students their first full course on Shakespeare, choosing to focus a major curriculum component on *King Lear*, a play that is, after all, built on the very foundation of authority. At that time I was preparing the play for an Australian edition[18] commissioned in association with Australia's Bell Shakespeare · Company, which is headed by the inspirational actor/manager John Bell (who will be the subject of this book's final chapter). I was new to editing and largely unaware of the extent of the task ahead of me. There is a full weight of scholarship born of double-barrelled names and lifetimes of detailed scholarly debate. Much has been written about the complexities of 'What – with the case of eyes?' (4.6.137), for example, and the mock trial scene in *King Lear*,[19] lines that Shakespeare probably wrote in a flash of genius and that have been shredded apart over centuries of exceedingly well-wrought scholarship. This was the field I entered in agreeing to prepare an edition of *King Lear*, the first woman ever to do so for a general audience. I felt my task to be ballooning by the minute.

As a way of bringing this project together with my pedagogy, I decided to involve my Shakespeare students in what was, at the time, an innovative electronic module. Working either in pairs or in small groups, the students chose a target audience for whom they were to annotate *King Lear*'s first scene. There were of course the inevitable motley-wearers (e.g. 'We're editing it for a group of lesbians, Ma'am'); but once they got started with an audience approved by me, the students enjoyed the process. They worked hard to embed their own interpretive bent while leaving the text sufficiently 'open' for their readers not to be confined to one way of seeing or another. It is difficult for busy officer cadets to relinquish the urge to rummage around for material that can heave them over the pass-line, and I did receive in their appended essays various assurances that Shakespeare was 'an excellent writer,' as well as a still-treasured reference to 'pathetic phalusy'. The act of making decisions about the text, however – of having the self-assurance to intervene through one's own glosses – pushed the students further and prepared them to think confidently and broadly about issues in the play.

The most powerful outcome of this project was the injection of flexibility it gave to the students. Through the editorial process the play became their *own* product as well as Shakespeare's. If you can put your own material stamp on a text, it becomes something that expresses parts of yourself and your world. Even more importantly, when students find a place of absorption in the play – a way of making it their own – they have a rich and legitimate field in which to explore complicated feelings and judgements. So, for instance, they may *want* a character like the irrepressible scoundrel Edmund to escape punishment or even to prosper. The Lear whom they have met in the play's first scene – addicted to his petty will, outraged by all challenges – perhaps frustrates or repels them. As they move on from their detailed involvement with Scene 1 to see him grappling with his losses and with the heath, however – stripping off his clothes to take on the garlands of nature, and ultimately bearing the broken body of his daughter to the stage – Lear's situation imposes increasing interpretive pressure on students who engage in the struggle to accommodate this 'unaccommodated man' (3.4.96). This is why drama is so potentially dynamic for students. It doesn't 'instruct' them to think differently – not even a self-help book can do this – but it offers glimpses, opens windows, lets the breeze stir feelings in ways they might not have anticipated.

Mullawah

Something else came up during this period and, although it involved only a few of my female students, it impacted my thoughts and teaching practices in a profound way, and impacted the students themselves as no course component could. An opportunity for teaching and learning emerged at a place called Mullawah, which is the Aboriginal word for 'rain', 'place of fog.' Mullawah is the women's prison in Sydney. Given its name, the absence of rainfall there is noteworthy. Yet, despite the fact that the location is quite sunny and the inmates are not required to wear prison garb, Mullawah is indeed a place enshrouded with profound fog and isolation. It is a place of banishment, a 'heath' of a kind, but, I will suggest, not necessarily the place of self-discovery that the heath becomes for Lear.

At that particular time in the mid 1990s the Defence Force Academy was awash in money. Lecturers were commonly required to teach a modest load of somewhere between four and eight hours per week, and had ample spare time to pursue other vocationally related projects. For some time I had been intrigued with the *Shakespeare Comes to Broadmoor* project in England, where theatre was brought to prison environments as part of a rehabilitative education scheme.[20] I had myself already gained, over a couple of years, a limited experience at San Quentin prison and the The Federal Correctional Institution, Dublin, places that provided opportunities to work voluntarily while I was at UC Berkeley for periods of research. I had also taught two classes at Long Bay Jail in Sydney, and had taken my students to assist with 'reintegrative shaming' sessions in Canberra, where a substitute for prison time was being tested.[21] Now I wanted to try something more sustained and ambitious, to bring a performance to a prison in Australia and see how things might work.

In 1997 I asked John Bell to use his eponymous Shakespeare Company to help me out with this plan, and he immediately agreed. He set about making arrangements for all of the security checks and paperwork required to have the Bell Shakespeare Company, as well as myself and my student assistants, go to Mullawah to do the full dress rehearsal for the company's current production of *Macbeth*. In the midst of a preparatory education session, a woman called Hillary[22] – an articulate, breezy person who was so purposeful in manner that at first I had mistaken her for a guard – said, 'I love the theatre. I saw a marvellous production at the Bellevoir last year.'[23] My face must have betrayed my surprise, because she winked at my students and said, 'We weren't born here, you know.'

Once Hillary got a taste of her audience, she took to the floor and things changed quite dramatically. The session had started off with a focus on *Macbeth*: but it turned out that Hillary's affinity was not for this play, but for *King Lear*.

> In a thunderstorm you suddenly understand how insignificant you are in the scheme of things, and then you're all washed clean. When I was younger I used to like to walk up to the edge of a cliff in a storm, and I'd get a mad urge to jump over . . . Now when I want to do that I get down and wriggle on my tummy so the mad person won't take over.[24]

The urge to jump over, the dissolution into madness, the overwhelming pressure of emotions that are too great to digest and make sense of: in a prison, one has all the time in the world to contemplate feelings too great to accommodate. But, in the darkness of boredom and personal despair, just because you may have the time to confront such feelings doesn't necessarily mean you'll want to. Inmates aren't like people in a distressing work environment. They can't just leave, try for a job with a publishing company or a pizza outlet. Even if they could, however – even if they were not cooped up at Mullawah – the striking thing about social rejection is that it relegates one to the edges of the earth even if one is actually at liberty to travel the earth.

Banishment, outlawry, shunning, and of course, transportation, have all been common forms of punishment involving ostracizing the offender. The Amish still do it. In Europe for centuries local communities used such practices to deal with wrongdoers. In some Australian Aboriginal communities, individuals who have committed crimes have preferred to face harsher penalties than white courts might impose – like spearings and beatings, for example – because otherwise the punishment would be banishment from their own communities.[25] More than ten years after I sat with the inmates in the bare, hot rooms at Mullawah, when I think of that place – in some ways probably as physically comfortable as many of them were used to in their homes – the deprivation they experienced emerges not in terms of things, but in terms of separation from the outside world. Others now controlled all of their connections with the outside, and others were there to enforce their banishment.

It is at the edges of the earth that, in our imaginations, we might find such inmates consorting with an old king huddled on a lonely heath. Lear's kingdom is gone, his home and his children, as are his 100 knights. All he is left with is a small band of social rejects. No matter what else *King Lear* is about, banishment is fundamental to its emotional plumbing. There is a sense of aptness that Shakespeare took me into Mullawah, this place of banishment, and that Shakespeare also helped me to contemplate what it was like on the inside, in the area of feeling. *King Lear* puts you on a cold and desperate heath and makes you stay there with the sufferers for a short space of time. In a prison, no one except the visitor has the convenience of departing after only a few hours. As an inmate you are there, for a year or five or seven – or even, very rarely, twenty-five, which stretches to the realm of the incomprehensible. This comparison between the duration of a play and the duration of a prison term may persuade some people to feel that my student assistants and I were no more than spectators of a situation that was our own prurient 'prison drama.' And there may be truth in this. But yet there was something we shared, an emotion we all recognized although none of us would name it: shame, the wretched infant's cry that roars up at a person from the inside at undefended moments.

Shame is quite different from the 'guilty' verdict rendered by a judge's hammer. Guilt is experienced because of what we do; shame is felt because of who we are.[26] Shame creeps into a child with the gaining of flesh and the lengthening of bones. It belongs to the place of unworthiness where one feels alone and rejected. In Lear it comes to the fore when he asks for assurances of love, and his dearest daughter responds with a grim measurement of obedience.[27] Lear has already said that he wants to crawl towards death 'unburdened' (1.1.39), but not in this way; and he doesn't expect to be 'unburdened' of worth as Cordelia's words so starkly represent him. He damns his daughter by Hecate and 'the sacred radiance of the sun' (1.1.107), summoning a violently expurgative rage to cover this place of shame.

In his rage, Lear tries to displace his shame onto his daughter. He cuts off her dowry and asks her two suitors who could possibly want her as she is now, 'new adopted to our hate' (1.1.220) and therefore worthless. She will be a living statue (as, indeed, Shakespeare, in a very different context, depicts Hermione in *The Winter's Tale*: Hermione is a wife who must be 'buried' as a statue for sixteen years while her husband is punished for mistrust and meets his own place of shame).[28] Cordelia, her father decrees, will be a lonely, penniless spinster. She will remind all of the court of the sin she has committed in rebuking him. But instead Cordelia is swept up by the King of France, disappearing from the British kingdom. And, divested of this 'new-adopted' warehouse for his shame, Lear must begin his own path to face a visceral emotion. It is his 'titanic journey' toward the inner part of himself – to the place of shame he has run from, the place that, when he reaches it, will mark his greatest achievement in preparing for his death.[29]

When Lear comes, late in the play, to beg Cordelia's forgiveness, it is possible for him to face the place of shame and to discover 'the import of his miseries' (Zak, 22). His journey has led him to see what he has feared – that he is indeed no more than a man. But this journey also shows him that being a man is enough. Hence he can finally ask, 'I Pray you, undo this button' (5.3.284), knowing that the place of shame is one he can now look at. He needs no furs or robes or even buttons to cover up his emotional nakedness. His nakedness is human, and enough.

Sitting on a chair with nothing else to do but be absorbed in a play – with the neat outlines of scenic division, climax and denouement and the comfort of vicarious experience – is a very different thing from crashing through life's vagaries as most of us do. But this is all the more reason why we might be moved by what we see onstage. Lear's journey to the truths he releases on the heath offers an emotional expanse in which it is safe for us to contemplate some of the things he sees. At Mullawah I realized, quite deeply, that not all humans can afford the journey that Lear makes to the face of shame; and that even if we do make this journey in our own lives, we might not always be in a position to understand it. We might stay out on the heath, starving and cold, and 'the heath' may remain a place of self-estrangement.

Lear has the Fool, Edgar disguised as Poor Tom, and Kent disguised as Caius, to help him make his journey, to remind him of the Majesty he is while showing him the frailty of his manhood – just as, in the subplot, Edgar stands at the cliff of self-discovery with his father, Gloucester, and tells him what lies over the other side. He thus helps his father to face his shame and to be able to say, 'I stumbled when I saw' (4.1.19). Can such love and support be found in a prison, somewhere you have been sent to with all the others deemed undeserving of mixing with humanity? 'Come, let's away to prison,' Lear says to Cordelia (5.3.8). Despite the old king's declaration that within prison walls he and his daughter can sing like birds in a cage and contemplate the magnitude of the world, a prison itself is not normally conducive to this kind of solace and renewal. At Mullawah you are removed from any people you have ever loved and trusted. You look around and all you see are mirrors of your own banishment, of the shame you try to push away, and of your will to survive.

In Mullawah, or in any locked facility, you have your story, and it becomes, however briefly and expediently, who you are. Your story is often a way of saying, 'I don't own this shame. I don't belong on the heath' (as, in fact, Cordelia doesn't belong on the 'heath' to which her father tries to banish her). This came home to me strongly one day when Hillary bustled into my class an hour late. She had had to meet with her lawyer to prepare her defence that she had been sitting in a dentist's chair at the time that 'her' crime was committed. But it was this return from the meeting that was so very intriguing. At first she could talk of nothing but the dentist's chair, the unfairness of the situation and the fact that it was all going to come out at the trial. But after another hour, when we were finishing off and the other women had left the room, Hillary was busying herself with the collection of various papers and pencils. I asked her about how her lawyer was going to handle the evidence provided by the dentist. 'What?' she said, looking blankly at me for a moment. 'Oh, that.'

My first thought was, 'How shameless!' Caught out in the weave of her defence story, she seemed not to turn a hair. But of course she didn't. In a prison everyone is isolated, banished from the world. And somehow, because you are human, you find, with the other banished souls, a community of sorts, although by no means a harmonious one. You have your story, and your daily plans and squabbles. These keep you in the here-and-now. Perhaps, for large parts of your life in there, shame is not in the front of your mind. Who can tell whether Hillary's story was true? But it defined who she was, for now, and it enabled her to live on her heath. In her private moments of self-scrutiny she may have exposed her soul on the heath, just as Lear does on his. Or she may not have. Hillary had nothing, it seemed, except those other souls around her, desperate to keep their own shame at bay, willing to accept her story of innocence if only she would accept theirs.

Our paths through the present and into the future are secured by the stories we tell of the past. The stories we tell do not have to be true – but they have to be coherent, sufficiently plausible to steer us through.[30] Our stories help us to gather together the threads of 'who' we are and to present ourselves to the world. Alone on the heath, or at the edge of the cliff, our stories can lead us towards the place of shame, or, indeed, they can lead us away from it. Without any of the supporters Lear has to help him face the place of shame, are we 'Lear' enough to confront our vulnerabilities and name them for what they are? And, for that matter, is Lear 'Lear enough' himself? The wonderful obliqueness of this play is that it suggests that the place of shame may be where Lear experiences both the depth and the limits of his own capacity to feel. He asks his daughter for forgiveness, yes – but does he have the vision to offer true caring beyond his own declaration of repentance and need? He doesn't tell Cordelia, for example, 'we must find a way to get you safely out of here and back to your husband . . .' The fences erected by Lear's narcissism may also define the limits of his shameful self-recognition, as he expresses his pleasure at having, at long last, Cordelia's 'kind nursery' (1.1.122), which is experienced all the more intensely because they are incarcerated together.

A Moveable Heath

I've talked about the way in which *King Lear* can distil one's feelings from the everyday in a concentrated kind of exposure. As I look back, I wonder whether, in a similar way, the prison might have mirrored for my students a familiar 'heath' where they lived. It is difficult to be at the Academy without feeling the cruel wind and the hunger for acceptance. Even in physical terms, the conditions for the Bell Company performance they attended were not unlike their environment at the Academy, punctuated by orders from 'outside'. During the performance at Mullawah a loudspeaker interrupted the action every few minutes with requests for such-and-such an inmate to report to the front desk immediately with permission to leave through gate three or four or five. The inmate in question would get out and climb over others' knees, ambling towards one of the 'screws' who would oversee her departure from the room. This evoked the environment with which my students were familiar, where their activities at the Academy at any given moment could be interrupted by an order to stop whatever they were doing and report to command. And during the classes I held after the performances, there were always incursions from outside, whether it be the late entry of an inmate who had just had a meeting with her lawyer; the absence of an inmate who had an appearance in court; or the effect of these incursions on the class itself, which suddenly looked, in the face of real life, quite trivial and even nonsensical. Who cares about Shakespeare when there is life to be dealt with, an argument to be prepared, a history to be revised, the infant's roaring within to be avoided at all costs?

Shaming people – making them feel contemptible and inadequate – is the special prerogative of closed environments, whether the occupants be the faded and slow-moving women at Mullawah or the young students at the Academy gleaming with health and enthusiasm. Prison inmates can be humiliated by apparent weakness, or for ratting on someone else, and they can be killed for the exposure of crimes that their fellows consider unacceptable. At the Academy, too – another closed environment – the internal regulatory hand of conformity can shame people, dumping on poor unfortunates all the fears and insecurities that others secretly feel about themselves. The pressure to adapt, to live successfully at close quarters with one's peers, to reach a pinnacle of physical fitness as well as to pass all of one's exams – these require a fortitude that some students can't maintain, and others more successful are quick to point it out. Being disgraced by an exposure of weakness (or weirdness) is a powerful mechanism of control, from the girl 'caught' wearing make-up on drill to someone who can't successfully finish a training exercise. Some few students at the Academy have even taken their own lives, having been forced onto the heath of 'outsiderness', mocked and despised. They are too young and inexperienced, and frankly too exhausted, to contemplate the heath with any equanimity. They see only the pit of shame, of deep unworthiness, and, very occasionally, a life becomes a secret found hanging from the roof of a bedroom, quickly buried so as not to damage morale or reputation.

In a prison you are locked away, regulated by your new community. There is no glass you can safely look into except to see the result of a prison haircut. I remember how surprised I was, after the Bell performance at Mullawah, that the inmates whose photos had made it into the press were thrilled. They were given multiple copies of the newspapers, and they taped the stories and photos all over the walls. I'd have thought that shame at being revealed as criminals would dominate their emotions at this form of contact with the outside world. But shame had no part of their reaction. Their negative ghosts had gone well into hiding. What they felt was a brief sense of belonging, and of *more* than belonging: for a shining moment they were celebrities.

'Allow not nature more than nature needs, / Man's life is cheap as beasts' (2.3.433), Lear cries with a mixture of irony and disgust at the depraved poverty to which he has been reduced. What *is* nature?, we might ask, and we will see the naked image of poor Tom, humanity at its most vulnerable. What *does* nature need?, this is a different question. The needs of an ex-king are very different from those of the beggar, Poor Tom. The needs of the students from the Academy – and the ways in which they can be humiliated and isolated – are very different from those that pertain to the inmates at Mullawah. But the mechanism of isolation is uncannily similar, and the mechanism of deliverance rises also from the same source. It is humanity – the sharing of moments, of a story of innocence that you don't question, of a long, hot morning – that brings comfort. One may not be able to escape the prison of one's circumstance or imagination; but one can, for precious moments, draw on others to take comfort from the perils of the pitiless storm.

'As flies to wanton boys are we to th' gods. / They kill us for their sport' (4.1.37–8), says Lear's mirror-self, Gloucester, in his misery. Having fatally misunderstood his loyal son and rashly depended on his bastard son whom he has blushed to acknowledge, Gloucester raises the question of how 'nature' is formed and 'who' looks down on it and monitors it. Maybe there is no alignment of deeds with deserts except in religion – and even in religion it is the gods whom we create that matter, not the gods who keep denying their presence through the operations of a brutal, uncaring universe. Regardless of how we view the structure of this universe, the prison system and the military academy create their own mini-universes that measure and regulate human activity through censure and incentive. But such structures have no framework for the longings of a human heart, for the ache of rejection, for the bitterness of feeling that one has been punished far beyond one's deserving, for the cry, 'I am a man,' 'I am a woman,' 'I am, or I was, somebody's child.' Only the gods can take care of this, and only if we believe in them.

The Orange Cup

Michael Jackson was one of the loneliest human beings I have ever known.

Ben Brafman, 25 June 2009

I said to Dad last night Michael's had his best years now. He was just a wreck. It's good that he's out of it and they can clean up after him. Poor man. Poor, poor man.

My mother, 27 June 2009

Loneliness is judged in proportion to wealth and privilege. There are many people on the street far more lonely than a King of Pop. They just aren't visible.

One hot day at Mullawah, Hillary offered me some water, and I said, 'Yes, that'd be great.' She poured water from the tap into her own little orange plastic cup, which was bitten all around the top edges. 'Here you go.' I was frozen, unable to decide whether it would be worse to drink from it and possibly contract hepatitis, or to put the cup down and risk a break in our relationship. I realized that no matter how pleased I felt about being at Mullawah and giving of myself, I saw in that battered orange cup a measure of Hillary's *difference* from me, with an intensity that I wouldn't have experienced had someone offered me a sip from their glass of wine at a party.

So here was Hillary, with her unknown background, her lack of hope, her possibly unknown diseases. Here was I, knowing that in two hours' time I would be returning to my middle-class life outside. And here was the cup, the thing that linked us for a moment more substantially than could any exchange of ideas – the bitten cup, my freedom, her banishment. Rather like Lear and Poor Tom, here, in this cup, was the symbol of our separateness as well as our shared humanity (we all need to drink). Lear looks at poor Tom and wants to talk with 'my philosopher', (3.4.158) transforming the poor madman into an object of his convenience while also admitting his connection to someone he has never connected to before. But Poor Tom is also at odds with *himself*: he is in fact Edgar, Lear's wealthy godson, who claims in this figure of the madman a cover for, and an image of, his lonely, rejected self. Edgar, like the madman, is banished. But unlike the madman, he is entirely aware of an alternative 'true' identity; he has somewhere else that is his 'real' upper-class life away from the heath, just as I had somewhere else that was my real life outside the walls of Mullawah.

Speculations like this can elaborate the problem of a moment, but they don't solve it or make it go away. I could philosophize all I liked, but Hillary was *waiting* for me to drink, eager to get me another cupful if I needed it. It was a small moment, but it is in these very moments that we often find images of the larger ones. The image that dominates Christian metaphor – drink from my cup/drink my blood, share in my food/share a part of my body. These images are not important for me as an image of Jesus Christ coming down from on high, because I am no longer an orthodox believer. They are the images of the true human commonality that the sharing of bread or water or wine can *stand for* – the embrace of humankind, one person sharing their humanity with another, the mixing of flesh and blood in the most common acts of our self-sustenance and care for others. The plastic cup, Hillary and myself, the repulsion at the thought of another's germs, the sense that my own world was so very different from hers, and that we yet probably shared dark places . . . Hillary had been sent to an environment where the food and drink she consumed was shared only with others deemed unfit for contact with 'the world'. But like me, like all of us, she needed to drink, needed a sense of kinship and belonging. The cup both divided and united us. I drank. And a second cupful. Hillary was purposeful and provided a third cup just in case.

Chapter 3
Playing the Fool

Speaking Truth to Un-power

As *King Lear* begins, Lear declares himself ready to be open to love and unburdened of worldly cares. Love at this point is clearly his *reason* for living: but it is the nature of love that reason can't provide it. Without love, faith, sex and art, life has no real meaning: and yet these fundamental human forces propel us into moments that defy all meaning. They are the traps that clamp the legs of men in high office; they are the unimaginable sacrifices that parents make for children; they are the miracles that make it possible to see death for just a moment, and to see life magnified through the glass of death. Lear's unreasonable reason – the yearning for a love that he has unknowingly debased – drives the play's first scene towards its shocking conclusion. When Lear begins to grasp the enormity of his mistake and cries out to Regan, 'O reason not the need: our basest beggars are in the poorest things superfluous . . . If only to go warm were gorgeous, / Why, nature needs not what thou gorgeous wear'st, / Which scarcely keeps thee warm' (2.2.434–6), he knows that reason cannot serve him. It is the Fool, and not his daughter, who he feels will truly understand the extremity of his emotional pain and turmoil: thus at the end of this speech he struggles not to weep, saying, 'O Fool, I shall go mad! (2.2.451).

Reason is often seen as the highest human faculty; and yet it doesn't touch 'the need'. 'The need' – the aching chasm, the sense of shame and loss – is very far from reason's capacity to understand or hold it. A Fool can understand it, perhaps, or a madman.

* * *

In the open, sunny land of Western Australia, with its large lots and expansive fence-lines, there lived a 2-year-old parrot, Boris, whose owner completed a military posting and needed to find a new home for him. He found a family willing to adopt Boris, who proved mild, even warm-hearted, a lovely household addition, happy to sun himself on the back porch all day while the husband and wife went to work, his casual companion their teenage son who stayed at home during the day and was seen to come and go. Two weeks after the bird's settlement in his fresh residence, an agitated elderly neighbour from across the fence-line came over one evening and said to the couple, 'Could you please control your son? He's very, very rude.' The parents were astounded that their son would have suddenly cultivated offensive public language, and, when confronted, he vehemently denied it. It transpired that the 'son' was indeed Boris, who had learned some spicy vernacular in his previous home. Once he got out onto the porch for the day, he would spend his time shouting to the neighbouring man and his wife as they drank their coffee on their own back porch, 'Shut up you fat bastard,' and similar things of that nature and worse. The discovery that 'the son' was a parrot changed everything, including the neighbouring gentleman's unhappy perception of his own portly girth. From that moment on, the elder folk couldn't wait to get out on the porch in the morning to hear what the parrot would say to them.

A motley Fool is not a parrot, but he may have the liberty granted to one. Like the bird, the Fool can speak discomforting truths, with the same license although with more purpose. The Fool's humour illuminates these truths; it intensifies them, and it also enables people to tolerate them by softening their sharp edges.

Who is the Fool in *King Lear*? He is a character of shifts, of chimeras, offering ghastly comic images of Lear's mistake and of its consequences. He understands and depicts for Lear the truth of his change in status. Dexterous and humble, he is a crucial part of Lear's movement towards renewal, though he is not himself renewed. All of the other characters in the play – whether they develop insight, or reveal hidden aspects of themselves, or disappear and return in disguise, or, like Edmund, prosper – can be seen in some way to expand and build. The Fool's trajectory is only downward, and his momentum in this direction can be felt, indeed, from even before his first appearance in the play. (Before the Fool first comes to the old king's side, Lear is told by a knight, 'Since my young lady's going into France, sir, the Fool hath much pined away' [1.4.62–3].) Despite being called 'all licensed' by Goneril (1.4.166), the Fool has the least political power of any character in the play. He can only watch his master helplessly, commenting on a state of disrepair that he knows will end in his own death as well as his master's. He declines inexorably with the sinking of Lear's fortunes.

When Lear awakens after his living purgatory to find that Cordelia has returned to his side, the old man says, 'If you have poison for me I will drink it. / You have some cause' (4.7.65–8). She replies, 'No cause, no cause' (69), a measure of love and forgiveness where measurement itself is no longer needed. At this point in the fourth act, love goes beyond all verbal limits and words are, in a sense, redundant. But it is the Fool who has embodied the meaning of love and loyalty long before it is pictorialized in this reunion scene between father and child. It is the Fool who displays a commitment to personal obligation, as well as representing the human *cost* of exercising this capacity. The Fool sees what 'truth' is, and he does not turn away from it. This is why Australian ethical philosopher Simon Longstaff calls Australians to be Fools: steady and unflinching in their exposure of truth above expediency.

> The Fool speaks the truth in the face of Lear's abuse of authority. The Fool speaks truth to power. He does it with humour. He does it at risk. But he speaks truth to power. And he pays the price, he is ultimately killed by the enemies of the King for doing so.[31]

As Fool this character might speak: but he is the Fool to Lear, not to Goneril and Regan. In this sense he plays the Fool in this drama not to power, but to un-power. By the time the Fool enters in 1.4, his master no longer has authority of his own. The Fool offers the Earl of Kent (as Caius) his coxcomb, signalling the foolishness of those who, as he does, maintain allegiance to the old ex-monarch. The Fool is a figure who mediates between the stage and the audience: he finds a way for us to care about the ranting old man onstage; and he provides a mirror for Lear to look at himself, since Lear's outrage – and the battle in his breast against the recognition of shame – do not yet make it possible for him to regard himself clearly. The Fool paints the comedy and the great sadness of circumstances in a way that Lear can bear to look at, but the Fool has no power to *shape* these circumstances.

Those who speak truth to power are unwelcome messengers; and it is a sad fact that while there are in the world many Lears (whether newly minted or long-time lived), these are far-out-numbered by the outcasts punished for speaking unpalatable truths. But the Fools who speak truth to un-power require a special compassion.

In the first scene of Shakespeare's play, Lear has given no indication that he has heard any truth the Fool might ever have offered him. It is only in 1.4, when the old man first experiences the effects of un-power, that he expresses any need for help in understanding his situation. ('Does any here know me? This is not Lear' [1.4.191].) Hence the timing of the Fool's first appearance in the play: Lear calls on him in 1.4, when he feels himself detaching from the web of hierarchical authority that has held him securely in place. 'Call hither my Fool' (1.4.66), he commands twice in this scene, as his oldest daughter's coolness is brought to his disquieted attention.

Once the Fool comes onstage to accompany his master, it is he who can ask questions that interrupt the severity of verbal measurements, opening Lear's eyes to his blind folly. 'Thou hast pared thy wit o' both sides and left nothing I' th' middle. Here comes one o' the parings,' as Goneril enters (1.4.152–4). The Fool loosens the locks on Lear's mind. He doesn't provide answers beyond his jesting riddles – he leaves the interpretive leap for Lear himself to make. We might see the Fool in a sense as Shakespeare's artist (his agent of creative 'authorship'), working in the play to translate and transform the single vision that Lear has of himself and his world.

The critic Winnifred Nowottny has commented on comic relief in *King Lear* as creating a space in which the Fool's tormented master can take refuge.[32] From 1.1 onwards the Fool gently buffets Lear with jokes and riddles that relieve the unrelenting pressure of his ordeal while illuminating the events that have set this ordeal in motion.

FOOL
Shalt see thy other daughter will use thee kindly;
for though she's as like this as a crab's like an
apple, yet I can tell what I can tell.

KING LEAR
Why, what canst thou tell, my boy?

FOOL
She will taste as like this as a crab does to a
crab. Thou canst tell why one's nose stands i'
the middle on's face?

KING LEAR
No.

FOOL
Why, to keep one's eyes of either side's nose; that
what a man cannot smell out, he may spy into.

KING LEAR
I did her wrong –

(I.5.14–22)

When the Fool teasingly reminds Lear that he has a nose in the middle of his face so that his eyes may 'spy into' truths he can't 'smell out', suddenly Lear peers through these riddles to achieve a moment of the very piercing clarity that the Fool is riddling about: 'I did her wrong,' Lear says (1.5.22), a bolt of truth that strikes him in the midst of the Fool's questions and observations about daughters and crabs and apples, noses and eyes. Following this moment of clarity Lear is immediately reabsorbed within the intensity of his suffering. For the particular moment of release, however, the Fool's riddles have taken the king to a different province, one *not* stuffed with the language of self-justification and suffering that characterizes such a lot of the old man's input into the play. In speaking truth to *un*-power, the Fool knows the risk and he sees the great wheel rolling himself and his master down the hill. But his words help Lear, in his newly disrobed vulnerability, to see that to which his power has made him blind.

When I look at my family, it is my youngest brother, Ben, who has become master of this art. In his growing-up years he sat on a little stool at the end of the family dinner table, quietly observing, learning to play the Fool but not yet ready to cross onto the stage, allowing us older kids to rock back and forth authoritatively on our chairs telling epic stories of eisteddfods and writing competitions and sporting teams (never relevant for me) and general school gossip. Ben's constant companion as a child was his imaginary friend Paul, with whom he would go fishing and to whom he would bring extra snacks, enabling Ben to grow quickly into his enormous hands and feet. Despite his size, he learned to make himself invisible, successfully persuading my mother for six months that he was leaving school early to attend weekly piano lessons, his cover only blown when my mother – too busy ever to have asked him to play for her – had an alarming encounter with the local piano teacher, Sister Walburger, on the street.

Ben waited thirty-five years until my father was a figure of un-power, retired from the pressures of the motel and the task of supporting his dearly and imperfectly loved five children. By this time Dad had the time and the vulnerability to hear the jokes that came tumbling out of Ben, who was unstoppable once he got a taste of what it is to play the Fool. Barrelling barbed gags at my dad like fast cricket balls, teasing him about his long-standing foibles, making outlandish plans with Dad for the speeches to be made at the old man's funeral, Ben is a figure of playful rebuke who is still always there to take my parents anywhere they need to go, to supply them with meals, a new bed, a new water tank. His truth – ironic, caustic – is spoken to a kind man who has never really understood the effect of his wilfulness on others. Dad is vulnerable enough to hear truth now, but too vulnerable to bear much of it. Speaking truth to un-power is a talent all its own. It requires empathy as well as humour, gentleness as well as uncompromising clear-sightedness.

Playing the Fool in Australian Public Life

Every culture needs Fools, and I would say that Australians are very good at playing the Fool. Our larrikin sensibility tends us this way. As a culture, we see ourselves as an under-class, living beneath the seat of power. The Fool is a natural figure for us, coming from under-neath to lift the lid on foibles and flaws and to challenge prevailing beliefs. The Fool can be dismissed as a mere fool while his truths find the soft place beneath the robes of majesty. This is his strength. His truths might never be seen fully, nor as clearly as they should be: but they come from a place of audacious creativity. It is vital for there to be Fools, whether they speak truth to power and ask the powerful to look to the future, or whether they speak truth to un-power and ask the bereft to recognize how loss has been incurred. There are scores of Fool-ish Australians to choose from, satire being a national sport. They come from all walks of life. There is, for example, anti-creationist Ian Plimer, a complicated figure who thrives on taking controversial (Fool-ish?) positions. While Plimar has lampooned creationist expeditions to discover the exact location of Noah's Ark, he has also taken a reactionary stance against the theory of human-induced climate change. 'Never argue with a Fool in public,' the *New Scientist* journal says of him – 'people might not be able to tell the difference.'[33]

If there is any 'lesson' that the Fool helps Lear to learn in Shakespeare's play, it is that value is found not in the words we use, but in the feeling with which they are spoken; that a heath is more than a place; and that within the most lonely prison walls he can, if he goes there with his beloved, sing like a bird in a cage. Late in *King Lear*, freedom is where Lear is with his youngest daughter. The kingdom that has been lost is restored in a vision of the plenitude of love before any formal bequeathal of land and rights (made in the final scene by Albany).

This image of true freedom and value was in 1997 offered in an Australian caricature, the figure of Darryl Kerrigan, a contemporary blue-collar 'king'. Darryl, the star of the movie, *The Castle*,[34] lives in a housing estate that remains undeveloped because it is on a toxic landfill, beneath power lines and directly adjacent to an airport runway. He rules his kingdom with beneficent oblivion, rejoicing in all of the discomforts and flaws that he sees as advantages (he is delighted, for example, that he can wheel his luggage on a cart to the airport terminal and get straight onto a plane with no need to call a taxi), and he is supported by his family in all of his whimsical pleasures. When the government tries to evict his family with an offer for $70,000, Darryl begins an epic battle to prove what he knows to be true: that value isn't in things, but in the worth we attach to them; that 'it's not a house, it's a home, you can't buy what I've got.' Darryl is the Fool: with humour and levity he feels truths deeply even if he cannot fully express them. He is also a cartoon Lear who feels himself 'every inch a king' in his outlandish castle; yet who knows that he is entitled to his dream not because he is a king, but because he is a man. And as with Lear, it isn't till Darryl is himself dispossessed that he sees the dispossession that has long prevailed around him. *The Castle* relates profoundly and explicitly to Aboriginal land rights and Native Title, which was (and still is) a contentious issue for all Australians, and which will be a subject for us to explore in Chapter 5.

The 2000 Australian movie, *The Dish* (like *The Castle,* directed by the Australian wise Fool, Rob Sitch), offers another way of playing the Fool to authority. Its subject is a true story, a giant radio telescope located in New South Wales at the time of the 1969 Apollo 11 walk on the moon. Its parabolic reflector was used by NASA throughout the mission to capture the weak signals from the lunar landing in order to televise the moonwalk to the world. *The Dish* follows three Australian scientists, Ross, Glen and Cliff, and their relationship with the NASA representative, Al, who is sent from America to New South Wales to help them. Al is contemptuously appropriate ('Enjoying your time here, Al?' 'Very much, sir. The people are warm and friendly,' code-words for 'dumb'.) As a participant from Abroad, Al authoritatively questions the way the coordinates in the NASA book have been changed ('This is unacceptable'). The young Australian scientist, Glen, admits that he has changed them 'cos they were wrong.' 'What about them was wrong?' demands Al. 'Well, they're the figures for the northern hemisphere, and we're . . . ah . . . down south. But I can change 'em back if you like . . . cup o' tea, Al?' The larrikin Aussies play cricket on the dish and are more interested in what is going on their pizza than in the timing of the launch. Yet they are wise Fools, their cleverness highlighted by their comical informality: they show that they can be laid-back *and* highly competent, poking fun at formality and living out the value of what really matters.

Some thought about the value of 'Foolishness' should also be granted to Bob Ellis, Australian humourist and political commentator, who has publicly thanked his mother for passing on to him 'a capacity for infinite complaint, which I think I carried on into politics and things'.[35] And Barry Humphries, the brilliant and maverick comic caricaturist, has nominated one of the worst things to have happened in his lifetime as being the broadcasting of Australian parliament on television, with its 'shattered syntax and garbled grammar'. Humphries makes fun of the 'tyranny of niceness and order' represented by the finer accents learned at pricey old-style Anglophilic Australian boarding schools as a contrast to the commonness of street urchin speech that predominates in Parliament. He cites an old joke: 'An English gent says to a stranger: "I say, old chap, are you an Australian?," and the stranger says, "No, just common." '[36]

The drive to take the stuffing out of pretence, to give the bitterness of truth the delicious edge afforded by humour, this suggests a 'Fool-ish' space that Australians delight in. But I think that Australian satire can also have the effect of domesticating or flattening complaint – of using humour, in other words, to provide a convenient outlet for lazy discontent. We can be bent double in rollicking laughter as we appreciate the antics of Humphries' ghastly female character, Dame Edna Everage, for example – but do we exercise our laughter muscle at the expense of exercising our democratic voice for judgment? Take as another example the very popular clowning incident played out at the Asia Pacific Economic Council (APEC) meeting in Sydney in 2006. The then Prime Minister John Howard was hosting all of the world leaders, including George W. Bush, to discuss the war on terror. Two members of the Australian Broadcasting Commission comedy team, *The Chasers*, Julian Morrow and Chas Licciardello, decided to bring Osama Bin Laden to the meeting ('If someone as stupid as George Bush can get a seat at the table to discuss the war on terror, then shouldn't we open it up to all the key players?'). Despite the millions of dollars spent on security for the meeting, the comedy team managed to get their own official car – complete with Canadian flag and a fake security number on the side panel – through all of the checkpoints, and 'Osama' stepped out and walked gently beside the car for some time before being eventually detained by the police.[37] The 'Osama' incident was a hilarious indictment of Australian security protocol and wastage of public money, certainly; but perhaps comic pot-shots like this end up illuminating, by contrast, the places that Aussie 'piss-taking' *can't* go.

Such places, in a play like *King Lear*, are those where ridicule is lodged in despair, where politicians are bitterly mocked for their 'glass eyes' that 'seem / To see the things thou dost not' (4.5.160–62). They are the places where disrobing – an old ex-king dressed in weeds – emerges in shocking counterpoint to the 'robes and furred gowns' that 'hide all' (4.5.155). The old man recognizes the counterfeit enabled by such robes only when he is himself no longer gloriously garbed, huddling on the heath as one of the wretches who were for so long subject to his myopic and dismissive governance. Disguise in *King Lear* is equally powerful, as it provides for both Edgar and Kent a means not only of self-protection, but of suggesting that we are *all* disguised. In essence we all begin as the naked babes that Lear hears wawling and crying as he struggles on the heath; and all of us must die. To live our lives with integrity is the challenge, when robes and gowns of various kinds make it easy for us to 'pass', *and* to 'pass by' those sights that disturb us. Both disguise and disrobing, in *King Lear*, are done by characters who are left with no choice – in order to continue with integrity, they must cover it all or give it all up.

Perhaps this play, with its brutal mockery and its liberation into searing truths, shows up the limits of conventional Australian 'Foolishness'. And yet, as I suggested in the Introduction to this book, no one can stay for very long out on a blasted heath. Satire is much less uncomfortable, and more fun.

The Fool in the Play, or the Play as the Fool?

In light of the previous section's closing comment, it is interesting that *King Lear* itself has often been used in Australia as a form of cultural satire: whether this be a satirical view of Australians or a send-up of the play *in* Australia is not always clear. Imagine the reviewer sitting at *King Lear's* first performance in Australia in 1837. Schooled solidly in both versions of the play that prevailed at that time – Shakespeare's version and Nahum Tate's much gentler rendition of the play's ending[38] – the reviewer recorded his annoyance at 'the click and slam of box doors being opened and shut', the general 'vulgarity of the people' that 'br[oke] forth' that night, as was typical with a full house, and the slovenliness of a cast that had not properly learned its lines: 'We could adduce instances of the almost total ignorance of their parts in all the performers from the first scene to the last . . .' But the crowning awfulness – the deliciously bad moment from which no actor could return for a decent lament about a dog or a horse or a rat

> . . . was when Mr. Knowles came on bearing the *dead* body of Cordelia (Mrs. Cameron), [and] an awkward circumstance occurred . . . Mr. Knowles could get no further than the words, 'Howl, Howl!' when *dead* Cordelia, perforce, laughed in his face![39]

In 1888, 50 years on from this debacle – and at the centenary of the landing of the first fleet and the founding of New South Wales – the Melbourne cartoonist J. H. Leonard depicted Sir Henry Parkes, pro-federationist premier of New South Wales, as a demented Lear crowned with a deficit and tormented by the signs of Queen Victoria's protectionist success, while his own colony (Cordelia) lay dead in his arms. The caption read, 'Henry Parkes, Poet and Statesman, R.I.P. and I.O.U'.[40] Whether such extremes of respect and gleeful caricature are 'special' to Australia remains an open question: but performances over the years have indeed often been marked by a form of situational self-mockery, as when, for example, Warren Mitchell came to Sydney to play Lear and remarked of his task of carrying Cordelia onstage in the final pieta-scene:

> There were three ladies there when I got to the first rehearsal – two tiny ones and a big one, and I thought, I hope one of the tiny ones is Cordelia. It wasn't, it was the big one.[41]

I am tempted to think of the 'big' Cordelia as a parodic symbol for the play that is so often referred to as a mountain to be approached

with trepidation and tackled with bravery.[42] 'What pop Lear needs is
a good men's group,' director Pico Ivor slipped in with his detailed
analysis of the play in the programme notes for his 1994 production.[43]
Somehow 'playing the Fool' is so intrinsic to Australian culture that the
very majesty of a play like *King Lear* – the very debt that we owe to
Shakespeare, whose great play has for many decades been set in so
many schools,[44] and stands as a cultural legacy with which most people
are familiar – makes us want to subvert it and undermine its authority.
'Because everyone's dead in the end and the play's really bleak, then
that's nihilism, apparently,'[45] says a contemporary Australian student,
according the play a bleakly funny kind of authority. Another
concludes after a school expedition to see *King Lear* in performance,
'I still don't understand why that old guy was running round in his
underwear.'[46] And a third provides a sample essay for the Higher School
Certificate exams, a choice excerpt from which is as follows:

*Title of Paper: Tanya Denny, director of the Harlos Production of
King Lear and Peter Brook, director of the 1971 film version of King
Lear, are having a discussion.*

Peter: Have you decided what approach you're going to take to
the play?

Tanya: Yes, well, I have been discussing it with my friends and
I've decided that I'm female and I think it's my duty to
take a feminist approach to the play. What do you think?

Peter: Hmm, Interesting. I'd like to see how that turns out . . .
It sounds good. I'm taking a more nihilistic approach to
the play.

Tanya: I plan to place a long picture of Lear's face at the centre of
the stage, but I want the picture to have no eyes!

Peter: I am going to have him strip down to nothing in actuality.
I want to emphasize the beastial pursuit . . . I was thinking
in the beginning of placing a fallice symbol at the centre
of the screen. [mis-spellings left intact][47]

I doubt that any of these three students will carry around for a lifetime a strong feeling of identification with *King Lear* (although they will likely recall boredom and covert laughter). But a memory of the play will be tucked away somewhere within their psyches, and, like many other ex-students, they may later feel quite strongly the intensity of moments like that shared with the whole nation by the former Justice of the High Court of Australia, Michael Kirby, who, during the early years of his tenure, made history by declaring himself an openly gay man, and drew on *King Lear* to express his emotion: "Speak what we feel, not what we ought to say."[48] 'Love transcends even scholarship, cleverness and university degrees,' he said. 'It is greater than pride and it's greater than wealth. It endures when all worldly vanities fade.'[49] This is the epiphany of *King Lear* – the simple presence of love, which does not need to be rationalized, measured or explained. An epiphany, but also a fantasy. Kirby reminds us, too, that no matter how we want to idealize its celebration of love, this play is yet 'a catastrophic story of failure of power and of human relationships, a thought designed to encourage the audience, as they part from the play, to embrace candour and to avoid idle pleasantries when confronting truly important matters.'[50]

Kirby's reminder about what's important brings me to another question about the role played by the Fool in *King Lear*. No matter how we romanticize the Fool's love for and loyalty to his master, the fact remains that he has given his life in a gesture of despair: 'I'll go to bed at noon' (3.6.188). The Fool goes to his death in the service of his octogenarian master who, miraculously, survives. Is one human being worth the life of another?, is a question that underlies the Fool's description of his own oncoming demise:

> That sir which serves and seeks for gain,
> And follows but for form,
> Will pack when it begins to rain,
> And leave thee in the storm,
> But I will tarry; the fool will stay,

And let the wise man fly:
The knave turns fool that runs away;
The fool no knave, pardy.

                              (2.2.244–51)

The question is also starkly present when a servant gives his life for Gloucester's sake after standing up to Cornwall, his own master – the only instance in the whole of Shakespeare where a character of low status engages his master in a sword-fight. Does the status and safety of the two old men merit the deaths of the Fool, Cordelia, Kent and the servant in the interests of their self-preservation?

Chapter 4
Polemics

King Lear, Action and Apathy

The question with which the previous chapter ended – what is one human being's life worth in respect of another's? – deserves further attention. *King Lear* depends on an underlying notion of regal monopoly. And it is through this monopoly that Shakespeare provokes us to contemplate the nature of human worth and deserving. Is a king's life extra-worthy because he is a man of power? What is a man without his throne? Do his emotions merit more attention than those of a man in rags? Lear himself asks this question in many different ways: 'Who is it that can tell me who I am?' (1.4.187); 'They flattered me like a dog, and told me I had the white hairs in my beard ere the black ones were there' (4.5.95–7); 'plate sin with gold, / And the strong lance of justice hurtles breaks; / Arm it in rags, a pygmy's straw does pierce it' (4.6.155–8); and, turning to the image of an unclothed beggar: 'Noble philosopher, your company . . . I will keep still with my philosopher' (3.4.154,158). In all of these ways, Shakespeare pits notions of assumed authority against the naked vulnerability of humankind. But for the effect and implications of this imagery, he depends upon the play's feudal structure. It is the feudal system of society in ancient Britain that folds into the play certain notions about worth: and it is precisely because this framework is there that we are asked to look beneath and beyond such hierarchical borders. Indeed, the play energetically encourages us to slice through the structure of feudalism and monarchical government, offering sharp critiques of the culture of power-through-property, and depicting the tortured Gloucester's quixotic dream of one day so shaking the money-tree of State that 'each man [will] have enough' (4.1.64–65).

The question, 'What is a person worth?' echoes throughout *King Lear* and into the current circumstances of Australians' political lives, in fact. Consider the national inequities in respect of human rights. There are sacrifices that Australians have allowed to be made: sacrifices of people in positions of weakness or servitude. There was the 'Pacific Solution', where in the 1990s a humanitarian crisis was translated into an apparent crisis of Australia's security and sovereignty, with desperate refugees from Taiwan represented as endangering the safety of our country, and, indeed, being accused of throwing their children overboard from the boats on which they travelled to a dream of safety; the policy towards temporary protection visas, which were in many cases in the 1990s withdrawn regardless of the asylum-seeker's connection to the host country; the neglect of immigrant support programmes; and, most importantly, the withheld right for indigenous peoples to have the respect and support of all Australians. In 1996, $470 million was taken from the Aboriginal and Torres Strait Islander Commission. Women's centres and youth programmes were shut down, and Australians were told that they could 'not afford' to help indigenous peoples who 'would not help themselves'. In 1997 the government released the Wik 10-Point Plan, designed to undo the native title act that had been established by John Howard's predecessor, left-wing Prime Minister Paul Keating. 'Someday soon the Howard era will end,' wrote academic and political commentator Peter Jull during this period.

Discussion of Aboriginal and Torres Strait issues will again be possible without cascades of furious denial and obfuscation from on high. The holiday from national responsibility will be over. I imagine the present as an Arctic white-out, or blank stage where a single actor stumbles helplessly, unable to find footing or direction, muttering, or shouting at Nature, like King Lear.[51]

It is not only conservative governments, however, that have stripped away the rights of already disadvantaged people: abuses of the weak have also occurred under the left-leaning watch. As I mentioned in Chapter One, we are a nation that upheld a shameless 'White Australia Policy' for 73 years in the past century. Even after 1973, when the Whitlam Labor government signed off on abolishing the policy, there was great opposition to Asian immigration by a party that saw itself as dedicated to the rights of Australian workers. And this went on into Labor's role as shadow government following Whitlam's dismissal in 1975, when the Labor Party was the centre of extraordinary racism toward yellow-skinned people pouring in from Asia with rumoured 'hidden gold bars'.[52] Herded together in Darwin, they were weak, starving, eager for a start in a new country whose public officials spread the story that we shouldn't let them in because they were hiding gold bars against their shrunken bodies. These were the 'poor Toms', the figures of need who were banished to the remotest part of Australia we could find. And as recently as April 2010 the left-leaning Rudd government, in a bid to curb illegal entry to Australia, halted all immigration from Afghanistan and Sri Lanka – even that of asylum-seekers. Quoting 'Thou whoreson zed, thou unnecessary letter' from *King Lear*, a blogger said wryly of this exclusionary tactic: 'The Aboriginal population of Australia might have wished the same measures were available to them a few centuries ago.'[53] And yet Rudd was in an untenable position because if he didn't impose a method of exclusion, the bulk of the Australian people would have started feeling that he was not securing their own welfare. Caught between a rock and a hard place, he was not unlike the Earl of Gloucester in *King Lear*, who finds that the old king is out on the heath but is told to shut up his doors. 'Shut up your doors!' (2.2.469) Regan's bold instruction, with a stress on every syllable, rings out as one of the harshest lines in *King Lear*. Cold, brief, emphatic. Ensure your own safety, and lock the grimness out.

While immigrants and indigenous people have felt the thin edge of the knife in Australian politics, workers have as well. Through the

1990s and into the first part of the twenty-first century, as a result of Australians' exercise of choice in three separate elections, Australia became a place where certain freedoms were excised as social rights and became privileges instead. Workers' involvement in unions became a matter of financial investment – an investment that many felt they could not afford – and media coverage gradually disappeared inside the deep pockets of privatization. Things looked and felt like Britain in the 1980s, when the doomed left-wing leader, Michael Foot, was likened to the broken figure of Lear in the face of Margaret Thatcher's brusque, coiffed efficiency. (It is intriguing to note that Thatcher herself has recently been given two links to *King Lear*, once as a tyrant and the second as the poor parent rejected by ungrateful children.[54]) Like Lear in the play's first and second acts, do we feel the impact of such events as an outrage; or, as the old man does later in the play, do we experience the outrage of inequity and abuse so intensely that our capacity for judgement is overwhelmed? ('This tempest in my mind / Doth from my senses take all feeling else / Save what beats there' [3.4.13–15]). Or do we shake our heads and say, 'Shut up your doors!'?

Flip Sides of Experience: *King Lear*'s Emotional Complexity

There is a reason that some people write plays and not pamphlets or sermons: they are interested in making drama, not in making model citizens. *King Lear* immerses us (sometimes over our heads) in images of human need, human brutality, human acquisitiveness, human self-relinquishment. The play deals in folly, regeneration, assertions of what is 'moral', and finger-pointing at carbuncles and devils; but it also abounds in flip sides that trigger strong emotions.

Look at Lear back to front, you get hubris against humiliation. The all-powerful king ends up with only patience to protect him against despair. Hence his appeals to *Homo patiens*, the New Testament's figure of Christ on the cross, the ultimate symbol of meekness and self-abnegation, of endurance against the force of fortune: 'Give me that patience, patience I need' (2.2.437). Lear and Gloucester offer flip sides of shame: Lear runs from shame in the very first scene, attempting to dump it on his youngest daughter; while Gloucester laughingly shames his flesh-and-blood and is himself later shamed and degraded. Cordelia and her sisters: the one who, as the play opens, is the recipient of benefits that have already been decided, the others who enter in acknowledged second place. By the end of this first scene the images have been flipped, the best-loved banished and the less-loved holding the keys to the kingdom. Edgar and Edmund, passive versus active. Edgar has, presumably, been happy to tolerate the inequity of his own entitlements in respect of his bastard brother whose birth out of wedlock entitles him to nothing. Enter Edmund, his flip side, who gets all that belonged to Edgar and still wants more. Edgar practises acceptance in dearth just as he has practised acceptance in wealth. Edgar and Poor Tom, played by the same actor, Edgar the image of abuse by others, Poor Tom the product of self-abuse. The Fool and Cordelia, flip sides of each other's truthful loyalty, the one banished because her truths are not tolerable or even understandable, the other Lear's close companion whose truths the king cannot avoid. Both flip sides meld together in Lear's image, 'and my poor fool is hanged' (5.3.280).

What do these flip sides do? They make excruciatingly good drama. They set up moral dilemmas and perceptual complexities. They offer back to us, in fact, the complexity of life. It has always been perplexing to me that humans require each other to be predictable in exactly the ways that human nature is not. A person who has great empathy can at times be impatient and unkind. A person with lots of money can still be dogged in pursuing a claim for reimbursement. The one thing that is predictable about human life and behaviour is that it will not follow a strictly homiletic path (until we piece it together in retrospect and leave out all of the moments that don't 'fit') – and yet we are forever calling each other to account for inexplicable conduct.

King Lear's elaborate pattern of flip sides explores this complexity and throws it back to us as Lear and Gloucester expose their poor aged heads to the thundering torrents of unkindness and the healing showers of compassion.

King Lear deals not only in flip sides of character, but also in flip sides of feeling, or, to be more accurate, in *under*sides of feeling. It has abjection, but not abjection without hope. It has love, but not passionate, romantic love – love as loyalty, love as restoration. The play has gods, too, but not warm fuzzy ones: they are gods to be sighed to in extremis, largely deaf gods who make Edgar hate the world's mutability that he yet has sworn to tolerate; heartless gods whose arbitrariness Gloucester decries. But the gods, nonetheless, are there, even if, as I suggested at the end of Chapter 2, we might have to invent them. The play has humour, but it is not a relieving humour. Humour, in *King Lear*, intensifies *emotion*, and the Fool inserts it precisely so that he can twist a knife in Lear's ruptured mind, exposing truths that Lear is finally open to glimpsing.

King Lear has often been called a bitter display of ultimate negation – a glimpse of redemption in love that is wrenched away by death. In the play's final scene, Lear knows deeply (but not fully) that a second chance will not be granted him, regardless of how he longs for it; that he cannot *will* Cordelia back to life, no matter how accustomed he is to a lifetime of command.

But look before this scene, and we will see that to have the reunion between father and daughter *at all* is a miracle of sorts, the flip side of the fact that Lear was blind and wilful enough to lose his daughter in the first place. Some parents never get even this brief miracle of reunion, living in regret and despair, or in angry self-justification. The embrace that is given in 4.6 depends not just on Cordelia, but on Lear as well. Lear is one of the most talkative protagonists in the canon, and yet, when reunited with Cordelia, there is a language shared that has a cryptic beauty. A father and his child, youth paired with age, each seeing themselves as an imperfect human, each marvelling at being found worthy by the other of the miracle of love.

And so, ultimately, when I contemplate this reunion, there is the question: what does it mean to come home? I have not been thrown out as Cordelia has – and for most of us, 'coming home' to a father is not necessarily about returning from exile. It is about sitting at the kitchen table with your parent, his face receding more and more, like an old satchel – and knowing that there is 'the bond' that Lear and his daughter have come to see the meaning of; knowing that as your parent moves towards the end of his life, you can be there at the table and there is love. Cordelia says, 'Oh dear father! Restoration hang / Thy medicine on my lips, and let this kiss / Repair those violent harms that my two sisters / Have in thy reverence made' (4.6.23–6). Her youth and his aged delicacy might move us to think of *her* as the one who brings restoration to *him*: but here she is hoping that he will give her medicine, and that he will be able to receive hers. She wants to be restored, and to receive forgiveness for whatever wrong she has done him. The most facile and oft-quoted line I have ever heard is 'Love means never having to say you're sorry.'[55] Love means being able to say you are sorry, and being able to have your apology received. Love is restoration, love is that moment of calm and strength when you know that you have both survived the storm – the atrocious storm that Lear has had to endure, or even just the storm of life itself. Love means you are home – both home. Shakespeare doesn't let father and daughter bolt the door and stir the hearth and live happily ever after; he doesn't even let them sing in their cage for very long; but still, for a moment, they are home.

* * *

'We haven't made love in a long time.' These words were spoken by my mother-in-law to her son as she woke up in her new 'home' in June 2010. After 52 years of living in her own house, 20 of them as a widow, the rapid onset of dementia had required my husband to bring her to a facility for the aged close to our home. My husband slept the first night in a bed just beside hers. He had only known his mother and father as people who lived as strangers in their house.

To think that she could turn over in her bed, as a 96-year-old woman, and feel intimacy for the man she thought was her husband, gave her son the chance to wash his childhood memories over with a feeling of relief – that there *had* been tenderness between mother and father, that there *had* been more than the endless fighting and the ultimate stalemate of disregard. Coming home, between mother and son, to a place he thought his parents had never been before – this was a gift that my husband could never have expected to receive.

Chapter 5

The Meaning of Words: Changing the Stage

> *Whoa, black woman thou shalt not steal*
> *Whoa, black man thou shalt not steal.*
> *Gonna civilize your black barbaric lives,*
> *We're gonna teach you how to kneel,*
> *But your history couldn't hide the genocide*
> *The hypocrisy, what is real . . .*
>
> *Kev Carmody, Aboriginal singer and activist*
> Thou Shalt Not Steal.[56]

Most people, either individually or collectively, have had 'power' that was subsequently taken away from them. The task of reparation, according to Scott Simmerman, is to undo the undoing – not to empower people, but to re-empower the unempowered.[57] In this sense, some version of Lear is in all of us, as is Poor Tom – both characters talk of power once possessed, and we see the effects of its loss.

No group of Australians has experienced disempowerment more chronically and collectively than the Australian Aboriginal community. Many Aborigines would say they have no memories of ever being empowered. In seeking to repair their wounds, therefore, we must create memories of strength that were barely ever there. But everyone *is* born, everyone *has* moments, months, years, in which they exist before the categories of life are hammered in around them. A king is a man; but a man might be a king before he is ever told that he is a beggar.

Why some must be given so little and others so much is one of
the mysteries that *King Lear* compels us to contemplate. This is
an extraordinary achievement, since the play is built on the very
foundations of privilege. *King Lear* gets us to look beneath and
beyond these foundations, to see the vulnerable places that privilege
has created and the need that privilege thinks it can ignore. In this
play, such places of need and frailty can't be ignored, because they
are experienced by a king.

From my childhood I remember, dotted around Oakey, families
whose kids would start to peel off from the mainstream community
once they understood what colour meant. Veronica Lawton, my best
friend in the eighth grade, who slipped into the shadows, recognizing
long before I did that she was half-caste, which made her black. Jackie
and Glenys Holmes, whom everyone insisted on calling Jackie and
Glenys French because Aborigines surely couldn't have a name like
ours. The black woman standing in front of me in a store, with the
proprietress looking over her head to ask me, 'Can I help you, Miss?'
Contrived as these memories might seem, they have not been invented
for the sake of a story. They were a part of my reality 35 years ago.

How *do* we appreciate the dignity of a people whom our forbears
thought of as subhuman – a people whose hunter-gatherer subsistence
was taken from them with their country? Eager to make their own
history, our forefathers rendered these people foreigners in their own
land. By the late twentieth century, Aboriginal Australia had been
largely whittled down to the few sad figures sitting drunken on city
park benches, chased away from residential streets and locked up in
jails, where they often died. Loss became their language.

In mid-2008 I was asked to speak on the 'Encounter' programme
for Australia's Radio National. The title of the programme was 'Giving
it all Away',[58] and the design of the producer and interviewer, David
Rutledge, was to consider how contemporary Australians dealt with
loss. He wanted *King Lear* to provide a thematic thread that would
run throughout the programme. Several victims of the devastating
2006 Canberra fires were asked to describe how they felt about losing

all of their possessions, and the interview material was to be inter-spersed at various points by passages read aloud from *King Lear*.

In my contribution as a *King Lear* scholar my brief was to describe how Lear himself interprets dispossession, and what the idea of his dispossession would have meant in the seventeenth century. I began with the observation that there is a huge difference between knowingly giving up the trappings of one's life and having them stripped away. And there is also a huge difference between the removal of your home by Mother Nature and the removal by other humans of your dignity and good name. Dispossession, for Lear, is not just about a kingdom: it involves pain, indignity and humiliation, and it rehearses the unavoidable dispossession to come in death.[59] Shameful dispossession ruptures one's sense of self and, at its most disabling, leaves people cowed and unable to move. But in Lear's case, as I mentioned in the previous chapter, there are characters who balance the old man's dispossession with reminders of who he 'really' is: an anointed king, and, in Act IV, a much-loved father. As Lear makes his tortured way through the play, the energy of the drama comes from the battle between his cognizance of dispossession and his capacity to cling for dear life to his sense of the figure he was (and is).

In preparing for the programme, the interviewer asked me to comment on any experience I had had with loss, and I told him that I had once faced dispossession of a personal and very degrading kind. Anger, an assault to self-worth and a sense of futility – these were the emotions that dogged my steps, and they are as fresh when I recall the experience today as they were those years ago. Emotional adversity strips bare one's layers of self-belief, and no matter how carefully you build them up again, in a gust of wind they can fly off, leaving you naked and vulnerable as you were before. This is the nature of such loss: self-doubt is at its core, feeding the emotions as blood does a tumour. When Lear weeps about his heartless daughters and calls them monstrous carbuncles, he is in part begging the ques-tion of whether he has created or deserved them, since a carbuncle is part of one's flesh. Can a loss take a toll on your heart if you are not in some sense susceptible to losing? Hence the self-doubt that remains. If one thinks of dispossession in this way, the title of The Radio National programme, '*Giving it All Away*', doesn't really apply. The title suggests a kind of relief in willingly relinquishing what has already been taken. The fire victims lost their *things*, but they did not have them*selves* stripped down to the extraordinary vulnerability that sets apart those made naked by an experience of loss.

When the programme finally went on air, its focus was entirely on the capacity of Canberra's fire victims to withstand their loss – of houses, possessions, precious memories – and their arrival at a belief that they could again build homes that had meaning. David retained my contributions about early seventeenth-century perceptions of the meaning of kingship, but nothing of my thoughts about the personal ramifications of identity-loss. I wondered why he even chose to keep the *King Lear* hook, since he so strenuously wanted to avoid the theme of personal degradation. The passages from *King Lear* read by an actor, David Ritchie, seemed like sonorous interruptions to a conversation that was really about how to handle the trauma of a natural disaster. Why did we stick so doggedly to *King Lear* if we were really there to talk about the personal impact of a fire? But more importantly, why stick to the fire if we really wanted to talk about *King Lear*?

In contemplating this question, I came to the conclusion that the very incongruity between *King Lear* and its application to the Canberra fires might say something quite important about Australian culture – something that was not in fact 'spoken' in the programme. It is central to Australian culture *not* to breast-beat about emotions like shame. Shame goes against the pioneering spirit. As I have mentioned at various points in this book, shame, unlike guilt, is a very internal emotion. We are not a culture that is comfortable talking about vulnerable states of mind.

I began to wonder whether the Radio National experience was more than just a fanciful textual premise on the part of a producer: to wonder whether the attempt to use *King Lear* as a consolation prize might expose a much deeper misunderstanding within Australian culture as a whole. On the day of the interview, *King Lear* was held up against the background scenery of ravaging fires: but the play can, in a different context, be held up against Australia's entire sorry history, revealing gaps not just in our empathy and understanding, but in our humanity.

Stretching all the way back to the arrival of the First Fleet in 1788, Australia has a history involving loss, shame, indignity and grief. The wounds inflicted on Australia's Aboriginal people are very raw, and for many years they were plastered over by a culture of alienation, ameliorated by crude applications of money allocated to 'fix' our racial problem. (Indeed, in the twentieth century people began to assert that compensation had gone too far and that Australia has been practising 'reverse racism,' conferring unreasonable advantage on the Aboriginal people: Australia's Liberal [conservative] Party leader, Tony Abbott, restated this view as recently as 2010.) Just the year before my Radio National interview, however, in June 2007, the Anglican Archbishop of Melbourne had spoken poignantly of what the word, 'unfair' really meant:

> Another aspect of Aboriginal life is the overwhelming grief that constantly embraces remote communities. In some communities of 1000–1200 people, it is not uncommon at any one time for 2–3 funerals to be planned, and people roll from one experience of grieving to another. I think the impact of that can't always be understood by non-indigenous Australians who only occasionally encounter loss in a close and personal way.[60]

As the archbishop pointed out, loss of this magnitude is beyond the comprehension of most Australians. So how *do* we acknowledge the Aborigines' loss and grief? And, more importantly, how do we acknowledge our part in causing it? It is this word, 'acknowledgement', that is the key here – acknowledgement of pain, acknowledgement of dignity and of the fact that in their degradation, the Aborigines were literally made to embody white shame. And yet for many years Australians had no language to describe this shame, choosing instead to see the Aborigines as feckless indigents who wouldn't look after the things we had given them and whose dishevelled lifestyles and homes degraded other people's properties.

I felt that in this culture of repression, *King Lear* might provide a way for Australians to imagine the scope and nature of these cultural wounds, and to talk about a part of our history that stores deep reserves of shame. This is what led me to start with an image of two unlikely companions in suffering: Shakespeare's old king, disempowered and homeless, and the survivors of a decimated civilization who, after centuries of abuse, might today well ask, just as Lear does, 'Who is that can tell me who I am?' (1.4.187).

We have become familiar with the idea that *King Lear*'s first scene turns on a link between language, loss and shame. Lear demands that his daughters give him expressions of love in return for portions of his kingdom. What he wants here is acknowledgement – he just doesn't know how to ask for it, and so he barters ridiculously with pieces of land. Cordelia's stiff statements of daughterly obligation engender an explosive crisis – in the court, in Lear's family, in the kingdom of Britain itself. Lear's kingdom and his identity fall apart because he cannot accept the words Cordelia gives him as a substitute for the acknowledgement he wants. This crisis in *King Lear*'s first scene can be very present and meaningful for Australian audiences who have lived through the 1990s and the first decade of the new millennium. In Australian society, too, a social and political upheaval was precipitated by acknowledgement requested and withheld.

Stories of pioneering history – like *A Christmas Card in April*,[61] for instance – yield depictions of stoic white men and women who worked the property and built homesteads on Aboriginal land that had been declared 'terra nullius'. Pictures of these homesteads are sprinkled with benign images of Aboriginal people dressed in little on most days and white smocks for Sunday church. My grandfather,

Ernest Skipper, went to Ravenshoe in Far North Queensland as a mounted policeman in 1926, and spent three years in regular contact with nomadic Aborigines:

> They didn't drink in those times, of course, there was no alcohol . . . You never saw an Aborigine the worse for drink, ever, not ever . . . There was always a bunch of them camped under the police station there, and the police sergeant . . . man named Lucy, was very good to them, very good to these people. We used to always give them two blankets each at Christmas time, and any old clothes that they wanted to get. Issued from the Aboriginal Protection Act, you know. They were sent there by the government for issue to the Aborigines. Never any trouble, lovely people. . . . See the Aborigines there [looking at a photograph], see the shack, the shanty they lived in? That's their natural, nomadic life, you see. That old feller [looking at a photograph] he never wore a stitch a clothes in his life. See, those ones would never come in for blankets, but these ones would come in and take the blankets back out for them. We knew them all as Joey and Tommy and Long Tom and all this, you know. We knew them all . . . never had a hair cut; but aren't they skinny? Poor little things, skinny, aren't they? Most of the people round there had one or two of them working for them.[62]

Camping under the police station on the land that used to be theirs, or around 'the middle stream at Vine Creek . . . another batch of 'em down at Perrets down near the Station', the Aboriginal people literally lay on the ground that was their 'heath', with policemen now patrolling their former kingdom. My grandfather would never have thought of this connection to *King Lear*, of course (and I am quite sure he had not read it). He recalled the Aborigines as 'very reliable'. It was the white people who were stealing cattle, forcing him to ride all night around the various properties and to sleep during the day in order to catch them. The Aborigines' nomadic roots enabled them to find a way of settling into the subservience required of them as they camped under and around white 'settlement'.

For many years, white Australians found it convenient to disown the Aborigines' right to their land and their dignity. They saw blankets and clothing as symbols of their own beneficence. As the twentieth century drew to a close and the Aborigines refused to die off or assimilate, however, they became more of a persistent nuisance, inconveniently reminding us of the abuses perpetrated by our ancestors. There were the decades in which Aborigines had slaved on the railways that snake across Australia's outback, or worked on white homesteads or as the 'black trackers' used by the police; the hideous years of 'Abo-hunting'; and the 'stolen generation', in which black children were taken from their families if they were 'white enough' to pass for Europeans and to be brought up as 'white', cleansed of the stain of their Aboriginal heritage. And, quite fundamentally, though their nakedness was covered by white people's rags, the Aborigines had been denuded of human dignity. Terra nullius, assimilation – two words that pretend that the Aborigines were never there. 'You are nothing' – this is a statement of ultimate degradation, worse than dislike, worse than rebuke.

Money is often used to quiet a wronged party, to acknowledge guilt while avoiding shame. The Aboriginal people, in the late 1990s, were no longer satisfied with money: as a people they wanted 'sorry', a word that would require white people themselves to look in the mirror and feel ashamed. The alcohol, the diabetes, the hopelessness that have wrecked many Aboriginal people – 'sorry' would acknowledge that these things were our shame, not theirs.

Two inverted situations lie uncomfortably together in my mind, in both of which acknowledgement is asked for: the one in which a powerful king wants an acknowledgement that he is more than his power; and the other in which a disempowered people wants a word that will acknowledge them as more than a financial burden to be disbursed from the coffers of authority. Two situations in which language connotes the emotions that go much deeper than language itself can ever represent. In withholding the word, 'sorry', the Australian government refused to give the acknowledgement the Aborigines sought. The government claimed that it was our fore-fathers, and not ourselves, who were at fault. Another version of terra nullius: our blame does not exist; your claim is nothing. We will give you money, but we will not admit culpability. The money without the apology says, 'This (objects of shame and need) is who *you* are; and we will not look to our fathers and claim that *they* are who *we* are.' But whoever has celebrated a national holiday – Australia day, the Queen's birthday – celebrates *who they are* on behalf of their antecedents. And whoever denies the word 'sorry' denies their existence as a part of history.[63] This is Australians' own experience of how families and nations can be affected by the freight that is attached to language. The experience is not universally the same; it is not felt even with the same intensity by all; but it is played out in its own way in our country and it has, in some way, involved everyone.

When Lear awakens from his ordeal on the heath, we witness a scene of heart-breaking acknowledgement. He tells Cordelia that he is unworthy because of who he is, and says that he is ready to drink poison for his sins. Just as Cordelia's 'No cause, no cause' can come only after Lear has admitted true sorrow and shame, so it is, perhaps, that the road opens for Australians once genuine shame has been owned, and genuine respect has been given and accepted. This was marked in 2007 when a newly sworn-in Australian Prime Minister declared white Australia's shame before the nation and the world. As a people we had grown accustomed to seeing Aboriginal people on their 'heaths', which had moved from the land outlying the police stations to the various parks around Australia's cities – places, smelling of urine and booze, where black people crouched in self-obliteration, waiting to fade away. In saying, 'sorry' to the Aboriginal people, white Australians came to the heath, making it a place that we shared in the ownership of. A place of shame, a place of banishment for far too long. Like Shakespeare's old king, who huddles with poor Tom and comes to see the abandoned, faceless numbers whom he represents (and who are just like him inside, no matter whether he is 'A king! A king!' [3.6.10]), non-Aboriginal Australians could truly look at the heath, the place they had designated as the Aborigines' land of shame. They could say, '[We] have ta'en / Too little care of this' (3.4.32–3), and really begin to mean it.

In the previous chapter I mentioned Hermione, who would soon appear on Shakespeare's stage as the emblem of another character's shame. In *The Winter's Tale* Hermione waits for 16 years in the shadows while Leontes journeys towards the point where he can see the hole in himself that he has covered by impugning his wife's integrity. Shakespeare, over these particular years of his writing life, was evidently fascinated by the shame that powerful humans[64] can displace onto those who have no power to shake it off. Four centuries later, Kevin Rudd said this same word, 'Sorry', and, like the long-degraded statue into which 'life' could still be breathed, the Aboriginal people were permitted to inhabit their own shrunken bodies again as men and women like all others. Many of their children were gone, their own lives had been sunken in despair – but there was still life and hope. All around the country, cameras showed Aboriginal Australians not bitter and vengeful on this day of reckoning, but crying, smiling, deeply happy to be called 'Australians' and to have their shame lifted from their shoulders and borne on ours. This is the miracle of humanity – that to say the word, 'sorry' can lift people away from centuries of outcasting. It amounts to more than pocketfuls of money, and pocketfuls of money can never measure it.

But, a skeptic might ask, is *King Lear* really 'up to the task' of addressing this complicated issue of Australian identity, fractured as it is, and torn as it has been by miscegenated language – language loaded for conservatives with one emotion, and loaded for the disadvantaged by another? Does the word 'Australians' end up still meaning 'white people'? Can we use Shakespeare's play to find a language that both white and black will want to use? Not really, I would say, especially when you imagine Aboriginal people, the original owners of a land now 'owned' by the queen of England, studying a play that begs sympathy for a British king whose land is taken away from him. *King Lear* is always going to be a part of white cultural heritage, an import from Britain that articulates the chasm between Aboriginal experience and the white person's world. The play will always be part of the scholarly curriculum by which white people (usually unthinkingly) exclude culturally different and alienated peoples. But if we can use *King Lear* (and I speak here as a white Australian), without having the presumption to impose it on a culture that does not answer 'father' to England, Europe or Shakespeare, then this is perhaps an important step forward. It is white Australians who have benefited enormously from interactions with the Aboriginal culture: going right back to those first fateful meetings in 1788, it is we who have come away with the land, the larrikin identity, the schools, the participation in a first-world sense of entitlement. So if we can use *King Lear* – which is part of our cultural legacy, not the Aborigines' legacy – to reflect back to us our blind spots, then the play will have helped indeed. It will have served as a form of connection, rather than as yet another means of cultural alienation that is imposed by the education department.

Chapter 6
Age is Unnecessary

What Does Four Score Years and Upward Mean?

A colleague recently mentioned that he had had a difficult spring. One thing and another happened, including his father's 'unexpected' death. It turned out that his father was 95. Although it seems ludicrous that someone would be thought to die unexpectedly at this age, still it is true that Lear's age – four score years and upward – though miraculously old in Shakespeare's time, is, while not exactly youthful today, certainly not atypical. The 80-plus age group today still expects many more years of bridge and golf and even tennis. It is also sadly true that medical advances have meant that there are many more aged bodies running around than there are sound minds to occupy them.

This raises a question that often seems to be missed in the drive to examine Lear's situation in terms of folly, sin and the possibility of redemption: how sound of mind *is* he? How much does his recklessness owe to the decline of age? In his opening speech Lear announces his wish to shake off the cares of his reign so that 'unburdened' he can 'crawl toward death' (1.1.39). The duties and obligations of kingship are felt to be a burden to him. After he exits following the banishment of Cordelia and Kent, his oldest daughter, Goneril, notes 'how full of changes his age is' (1.1.284), adding, 'The best and soundest of his time hath been but rash' (1.1.290). The first scene therefore leaves it very unclear as to whether we are dealing with a fully capable and culpable character who has always been impossibly headstrong, or with someone thrashing in his dotage.

This accentuates our interpretive dilemma in just the same way as we find when we are dealing with an aged parent who has always been cranky. Is manifest unreasonableness simply what has long prevailed, or is it symptomatic of the age that is 'full of changes'? Should actions be judged on a medical or a characterological basis? And if the former is true, then the person is not responsible to govern his/her affairs, and the obligation to do so should be removed (just as Regan indicates when she says, 'Oh Sir, you are old . . . You should be ruled and led / By some discretion that discerns your state / Better than you yourself' (2.2.314–15).

It might be surprising to find that in Australia the issue of elder care has been given the occasional label, 'The *King Lear* syndrome'. The questions concerning the infirmity of Lear's age entail loss of judgment, loss of control and loss of dignity – the loss of authority over others, and often a diminished capacity to 'author', or control, oneself. How do we value age when its material usefulness has been superseded and has often indeed gone backward? Ruth Wajnryb writes in *The Sydney Morning Herald*:

> After all, the old are closer to the end point. Closer to death's door. English is replete with euphemism: we insure against death but call it 'life insurance'; we 'pass away'; we're processed by 'morticians' and 'undertakers'. We dread the suggestion to 'get your affairs in order'. King Lear said it best, when the Earl of Gloucester pleaded to kiss his hand: 'Let me wipe it first; it smells of mortality.'[65]

When Shakespeare's Lear asks his suffering doppelganger Gloucester to allow him to wipe his hand first because it smells of mortality (4.5.126), mortality refers to a condition that was understood by people of Shakespeare's time – it was an integral part of everyday life, and Lear could be seen to have had double his expected innings. And yet, despite the presence of mortality everywhere – in the signs of the plague, for instance, in the high rate of infant and maternal death, even in the complications of a common cold – Lear's words about the smell of mortality bear a potent sense of fear and denial. He does not want to be old and unloved; he talks of crawling towards death, but he wants to be accompanied. In today's first-world societies, fear and denial are all the more present because, while we understand even less about what happens to us after death (people in Shakespeare's time at least believed in heaven universally), death is now something we hardly want to think will happen to us at all. But mortality looms all the larger today because of the sense of loss, the diminution of power, that afflicts a future-oriented population. So, in a sense, we are a society that increasingly understands what it might feel like to be Goneril, Regan and Edmund, and to fear what it is like to be Lear or Gloucester. Deemed unattractive and redundant to busy nuclear families, age is superfluous. When should we start to apply a cost-benefit analysis to a new pair of shoes, or a coat, or a bottle of perfume, given that their usefulness may long outlive the life of the person they are purchased for?

The very recent downturn in the global economy (commented on in a recent Australian economics blog with a reference to 'an enigmatic Lear-style trillion dollar [rescue] plan'[66]) as well as worldwide cuts in social services, have meant that many mid-life Australian people are compelled to confront the problem of their aged parents. They are choosing, with greater or lesser degrees of hesitancy, to care for parents whom they might previously have sent off to pricey nursing facilities. These younger people might also have delayed child-bearing until later in life, so that it is not uncommon for the mother of a 4-year-old, for example, to find herself bathing her child and her mother in the one afternoon.

I have two mothers-in-law, one my husband's mother and the other the mother of his deceased wife. One is 96 and the other 97. On the occasions over the past few years when I have helped my husband's mother to shower, I am moved by the combination of complete concentration, vulnerability and trust involved in the endeavour. There are things she knows she can't do, like scrubbing her own back, for example. But there are other tasks – like drying her feet, toe by toe – that she hangs onto for dear life, fearing that to relinquish them once will most likely be to relinquish them forever. One can feel enormous love and compassion for the old person who has had to become a child again. Sometimes such a person has little recognition of what can't be achieved alone anymore. But some elderly people do feel unmistakably the ebbing of their faculties, knowing what this means, and they suffer for the limitations that pull reluctant children closer. My husband's mother allows me to help her, understanding that, with physical and mental decline, privacy is a luxury that safety can no longer afford. But what would it have been like if she'd accepted the care shown by my husband and me while deciding to leave her remaining assets to the next-door neighbour, which is her legal right? In a small child we can find it charming to see the endless demands placed on relatives who are also required to buy handcrafted paintings for a dollar. But in an elderly person – someone who should have come to understand the tacit contractual relationships that evolve around duties and possessions – the seventh age of man can seem hideously rash. It can be difficult to wipe the bottom of a crabby parent who has decided that all such favours are fully paid in advance.

It is fast becoming a possibility in contemporary Australia that people in mid-life will feel compelled by financial laws to choose between putting their elders in nice retirement homes and putting their kids through college. Welfare services are being cut and reshaped, and residents in elder homes may in the future, as in America, be required to spend their way through their assets before relying on the state for subsistence. Citing the burden this puts on families and their elders, a 78-year-old quotes from *King Lear*: 'He hates him who would on the rack of this rough world stretch him out longer . . . There are surely ways to prevent voluntary euthanasia not being abused . . .'[67] But in general the reduction of social welfare programmes, and the decline of the extended family tradition, has put fear into elderly people – fear of being constrained to let things end quickly in the interests of expediency, fear of being thrown away. This has encouraged many to hold onto their money rather than disbursing it among their beneficiaries. *King Lear* can prompt us to reflect on one of the tenets of human nature – the fact that no matter what one gives, once it has been given the beneficiaries no longer see it as yours. They see it as theirs, and they often resent or deny the obligation that a gift of property might incur.

The title of 'Lear' has been attached to such famous Australians as Rupert Murdoch and Len Ainsworth (both of whom have distributed their properties among family members in ways that have caused family ructions),[68] and to figures as disparate as anthropologists and rugby coaches in the context of a generalized assignation of mad redundancy.[69] But the Lear syndrome remains a concern with particular ramifications for people on Australia's rural properties. They might not have the physical strength to continue their work on the farm, but they feel fully able to retain control of the work that is done by able-bodied family members. 'The *King Lear* syndrome', says John Longworth, 'is understandable' in this rural context.[70]

Life on a farm is such that a man can continue to participate in the family business well past the usual retirement age. The pre-death transfer of the power to make decisions is, therefore, difficult for the aging farmer to accept because he often, rightly or wrongly, sees his long experience on the family farm as the paramount qualification required for good managerial decision-making. His experience is a heart-breaking one, as he stands alone, skin baked by the sun (perhaps with his long-suffering wife), at odds with the reality of modern technological progress. If he won't let go of the farm, however, his children are forced to go along with his resistance to change, engendering inflammatory family circumstances as the economic situation of the family falls apart. Elderly farmers, having lived on a farm for 50 years, and having bought up properties that are now barren, might face a brutal choice. Do they hand these properties over to children who will utterly change the way they have always been run? Do they walk away from properties they can no longer maintain, hoping that they might recover their value later? Or do they hang on?

Mute endurance is the image that comes to mind here – the bonds to the land that are deep beyond words, and the truth that no words can fix anything. 'Men must endure / Their going hence even as their coming hither' (5.2.9–10), says Edgar in *King Lear*. But it might seem easy for a young man to talk of coming and going, since going is for him a long way off. The oft-repeated 'patience', described in Chapter 4, is in *King Lear* a word that screams quietly of the cost of loss, when there is little left but to beg strength to bear suffering. 'I will be the pattern of all patience. / I will say nothing' (3.2.36–7). For the old, worn Australian farmers who come to exist as the detritus of life, there is often little or nothing to say.[71] There is really no rejoinder to the brutal clarity of Edmund's declaration that he owes his father nothing, and that his father, being old, has had his time. In fact, his frailty is itself a timely cue for the emergence of the strong: 'The younger rises when the old doth fall' (3.3.22).

Unburdened Crawling towards Death . . . Playing It on Stage and Page

What is it about Lear's ordeal that earns him the term, 'tragic hero'? There is some kind of greatness, some sense of what has been lost and of the degradation that one has been reduced to. Writing just after the Second World War, Australian actor/manager John Alden speculated in response to Charles Lamb's belief that the agony of *King Lear* makes it an unsuitable (and even indecent) play to watch onstage: 'The modern mind tempered by two world wars does not find *Lear* too unbearably cruel. In point of fact, I can imagine that some people find the spiritual regeneration of Lear and Gloucester rather comforting.'[72] The 'tragic' note in any depiction of these two characters depends, indeed, on the degree to which they display the capacity to recognize and to rue their own folly. There is a limit to how tragic you *can* make an aged madman who isn't at all bothered about what he used to be.

Interestingly, in 1998 Barrie Kosky directed a production of *King Lear* that altogether mocked the notion of the play as tragic. This production suggested that the end of life 'means' nothing – that Lear is a gabbling fool, surrounded quite appropriately by vaudeville incontinences and nonsensical loudness. I'll mention this production in more detail in Chapter 7 – but for now I want to draw from it one of the most moving and, in a sense, inexplicable, scenes I have witnessed in the theatre. We were taken, after interval, to a bus-station setting. Alone amidst a scattering of ragged orange plastic chairs, John Bell, as Lear, absent-mindedly tore a piece of paper into scraps, dropping the scraps on the floor and chattering out his lines. This was a Lear who had lost everything, including his mind, and did not redemptively or instructively get it back again – a Lear who shadowed the many thousands of faceless figures in contemporary society, people whose assets they have willingly or unwillingly given away, and who are living with low cholesterol levels and shrunken brains, perhaps not even able to acknowledge the misery they have been reduced to. This Bell/Kosky Lear scene displayed a state of being, a form of incognizant subsistence (not endurance, since this term implies an effort of will). Lear sat, bewildered, in an old bus station, his senseless chatter marking the fact that he was still *there*. This was, for the moment, what humanity amounted to.[73]

Some Australian writers have been inspired by *King Lear* to depict the dilemmas surrounding the burdens of age. David Williamson's play, *Travelling North*,[74] was performed all around Australia in 1979 and filmed in 1987. The 'hero' of *Travelling North*, Frank, is plagued by an ailing heart in his twilight years. Eager for a last lease on life, he has met up with Frances, a younger woman who, like Frank, struggles, attempting to reevaluate her broken marriage and her relationships with her children. Frank and Frances decide to move up north, where Frank soon descends into self-absorption, treating Frances as an unpaid servant. What makes him behave like this? And why does she put up with it? As we share glimpses of their past, we are left to answer these questions for ourselves.

A man with a lifetime of authoritarianism behind him, Frank is a local Lear who refers to Frances' daughters, Helen and Sophie, as 'Goneril and Regan . . . As soon as I've gone they'll have you down on your knees scrubbing floors again,' he tells Frances (p.61). However, as his history of misogyny emerges with increasing vividness, any Machiavellian impulses in Frances' daughters pale in comparison with the old man's self-involvement. In the course of the play Frances temporarily leaves Frank, and, like Lear, he comes to the glimmering understanding that his actions might not match his motives. 'While I've always loved mankind in general, I have been less than generous to some of those I've been involved with in particular,' he observes to Frances' daughter Joan (p.56). But even this painful understanding is more self-serving than self-revealing, as he later parrots it to Frances in an effort to induce her to return to him. As with Lear, we are left wondering how much Frank really understands about himself and his effect on others. And we are given no more assurance about Frances' character either. Quick to blame herself for having farmed out one of her daughters at the age of eight, Frances is now trying to embrace responsibility instead of rejecting it. But as her daughter Helen points out, it is she and her sister to whom Frances owes responsibility, not a man whom she has only recently met: 'Just when she's starting to help us a little, she runs off without a word of warning' (p.14). And in an echo of Cordelia's loyalty to her parent, Helen, we learn, sends Frances cheques all through her years with Frank, thereby enabling her mother to sustain the relationship that she herself resents.

Thea Astley's 1994 novel, *Coda*,[75] is built around a distinctly Lear-like anti-heroine, Kathleen. Sometimes with trenchancy, sometimes with humour, sometimes with rage, Kathleen insists that age cannot be swept under the carpet. Each part of *Coda* begins with a newspaper article describing elderly people – unidentified and unable to identify themselves – left sitting or wandering in public places. These articles bracket a three-part story in which the elderly protagonist tries to 'identify' a self that is awash within her memories and her ungrounded present. In Part One we see Kathleen living alone and sorting through the 'brilliant sharp-edged pictures smashing against memory' (p.15). After she goes to the mall and gets lost, she turns to her children, Sham and Brian, for help. Brian has just got rid of her from a visit, and guiltily hopes that Sham will know what to do with her. Sham and her husband won't take her in, and they book her into a retirement village called Passing Downs. She lasts there for two nights, disturbing the peace very badly. In Part Three, our last glimpse of Kathleen is of her wandering the city (her urban heath), talking with her dead friend Daisy, being mugged, and, at last, planning a literal and metaphorical trip to 'the island'. She waits impatiently for Daisy to join her ('Trust Daisy to be late!' [p.186]), and has to step onto the ferry alone.

Astley's novel has a split surface. On the one hand life looks nightmarish for the spirited old woman who is determined not to go quietly. Nobody wants her, and nobody – not even the government, which plans to build a road through her house – is inclined to make allowances for her. Age is in the way, and must be disposed of. Visiting a hall of mirrors, she says impatiently to the guide, 'My turn . . . my turn.' When the guide leads her to the glass, however,

she looks in the mirror [and] it is milky, purblind, the surface of a pallid emulsion that washed sluggishly within the frame. *What's this then?* She asks the guide, who is shuffling his feet. *Don't I get a look? That's it, lady,* the guide says.

But even though everyone and everything in her life – even the hall of mirrors – conspires to make her disappear, Kathleen, 'rendered invisible . . . by her very age' (p.175), insists that her 'self' does matter. As her control lessens and her faculties are increasingly limited, yet she continues her determination to live, and not to be ashamed of still existing.

In Helen Garner's 2008 novel, *The Spare Room*,[76] the protagonist, Helen, invites her old friend Nicola to stay in her spare room while 'recovering' from a cancer treatment. The novel is steeped in dramatic irony: despite all of the evidence available, Nicola herself is the only person who seems not to accept that she is on the way out. She tortures her body with expensive new-age treatments, and burdens Helen with a visit far longer than initially planned, forcing her into the position of nurse for a pitifully frail and incontinent body. What is most present about Nicola is sheer ego, the refusal to go down gracefully. Unlike Lear, however, Nicola has no trajectory towards pitiable self-revelation: she simply runs out of options but not before Helen runs out of patience. The novel presses triggers for an Australian Lear-like dilemma: how do we suffer the suffering when their trials are so burdensome to others as well as to themselves? But Garner's narrator is no Fool and no Caius, implicitly asking her readers to judge what is more distasteful – Nicola's extreme self-absorption (her unremitting will to live which blinds her to the burdens she places on others), or the frustration with which the narrator depicts Nicola's situation. *The Spare Room* is the closest contemporary Australian novel I have read to something I might attribute to Regan or Goneril: in the end, the narrator suggests that her unreasonable female 'Lear' doesn't know when to say 'die'.

All three of these contemporary Australian pieces draw on *King Lear* to ask the question: what will we do with the aged? And this question is only more pressingly superseded by another, as the protagonists themselves ask: 'What do I do with myself? How do I manage this unknown path when I don't want to call its end point "death?"' Those in decline still often have hope, and, while it may look foolish or misguided to the able-bodied, this doesn't mean it has no right to exist. Nothing can stay the same, and this is the battle that we have as we age – to give way to the young while being cognizant of the meaning that resides in the past; and to draw enough sustenance from the past to feed what future remains. Living on the (emotional and financial) proceeds of the past doesn't mean that one has no right to imagine a future.

In *King Lear*'s final scene, Lear stumbles onto the stage with his daughter in his arms. He knows that she is dead: he knows too well *and* he knows not well enough. How much of his daughter can be lost while her essence still remains? There is death, and there is also the impossible hope that feeds the imagination. Lear's kingdom may have been restored to him by Albany, but this means nothing to the old man now. Hope is his kindle – whether it be hope that Cordelia is still breathing here with him, or hope that he can join her: 'Look there! Look there!'

I know that this image is fuelled by my own imagination, just as Cordelia's image is fuelled by her father's hope. In many times and places in the world, dead bodies are not viewed with such awe and attention, and, indeed, may simply be seen as a putrefying nuisance. A friend of mine went from Australia to Papua New Guinea 20 years ago and found a dead body by the side of the road. No one – at the hospital, the morgue, the police station or the coroner's office – would accept the body because it didn't have any papers. At the end of a long evening of driving he felt compelled to return the body to the side of the road. In this sense, Cordelia and Lear have a rather lovely departure because the one is longed for and the other reverenced, and both are publicly mourned.

Chapter 7

The Man as the King, the King in the Man

'To respond with compassion', writes Martha Nussbaum, 'I must be willing to entertain th[e] thought that this suffering person might be me.'[77] In order for the impossible brutality of *King Lear*'s action and the misogynistic, self-centred rantings of the aged protagonist to have emotional resonance, the character has to be someone whom we don't just theorize about, but *care* about. And ultimately, this book has argued that we are asked to care about Lear as a character not because he represents a theological or political ethos, nor even because he is a king who has been 'dis-graced': we care about him because he is someone who has lost everything, who comes to see that he was deluded and that the self he was forced to discard was not a true self at all. In the course of the play he finds a truer self, though not without struggle and not without backsliding.[78]

This old man, this father, embraces his folly as he embraces the daughter he once threw out of his house. Through his diminishment he learns to grow, and to *see* the things of which he has 'ta'en too little care' (3.4.32–3). He finds that love can be regenerative in the very way that a miracle is inexplicable. Love might not come in the way you once thought it would, and it will not come forever; but it can still come, and you can still be comforted by it.

An actor isn't a piece of hose that connects the dramatist's mind with the collective mind of an audience: every time *King Lear* is performed on stage, the specificity of the context plays its own particular part in shaping the 'Lear' who emerges. Society is changing and Shakespeare's play stays the same: but the very *difference* in each production highlights the unique collaboration between play, place and player. In this final chapter I will shine a light on actor-manager John Bell (officially appointed in 1997 by the National Trust of Australia as one of the country's Living Treasures), who will serve as a yardstick to gauge the recent texture of Australian society as it comes into view around performances by a particular man who has, in three different decades, played the role of Lear in three productions.

John Bell has spent his life as a Shakespearean actor and director, performing in a one-man Shakespeare production at the age of 22 and joining the Old Tote Company the year after. That same year he founded the 'Three Bob Theatre', a lunchtime Sydney theatre company. At the age of 25 he travelled to England to join the Royal Shakespeare Company and was appointed as an Associate Artist the following year. Three years later, just before turning 30, he joined Philip Hedley's company at Theatre Royal, Lincoln, and the year after that he returned to Australia as the head of the National Institute of Dramatic Art (dramatic birthplace of Colin Friels, Mel Gibson, Baz Luhrman, Cate Blanchette, Judy Davis and Toni Collette). For the next 15 years Bell worked with several theatre companies, including the Nimrod and the Old Tote. In 1990 he founded the Bell Shakespeare Company, which has become one of the most prominent theatre companies in Australia's history. Bell first played the role of Lear with the Nimrod Theatre Company, and the last two productions have been with his eponymous company.

The 1984 *King Lear*: 'Nothing can come of nothing'

'I've got nothing against Aboriginals, but you wouldn't want to live near one, would you?' By 1984, conservative Queensland Premier Joh Bjelke Petersen was well into his 70s, and had been leaving his mark over Queensland for 16 years – through my early childhood years and right through my period at university and beyond. He spoke of news conferences as 'feeding the chooks', said of human rights, 'What's the ordinary man in the street got to do with it?,' and complained, 'The trouble is that Queensland gets branded as part of Australia.'[79] At Queensland University, the flashing lights of Queensland police cars were a regular sight as policemen came in to carry off civil rights protestors. Along with the rest of liberal Australia, I laughed at Joh's malapropisms; but if I had not been so preoccupied with my own youthful affairs I would have stopped (I should have stopped) and gone to jail with them. Joh would never look at the needy and say, 'I have ta'en too little care o' this.' He would say they were malingerers and plan a road to cut through their rental properties.

Joh appealed to the pioneering spirit of a people who had grown up, over the past two centuries, in the 'school of hard knocks', and who did not want to surrender any of their freedoms to the social welfare offices. Regardless of this strongly conservative Queensland vein, however, things were beginning to change around Australia as the economy boomed. In 1984, Prime Minister Bob Hawke brought back into effect all of the key points and benefits of the Medibank plan that had been drafted by the sacked left-leaning Whitlam government almost a decade earlier. Renamed Medicare under the Hawke government, this health plan was able to cover every human being in Australia in a nationalized health system.[80] The Native Title restoration of land rights to Aborigines, drafted by the Whitlam government in 1975 and implemented by the Fraser government in 1976, had been operative for several years. As well as this, in 1983, voting had been made compulsory for Aborigines, as it was for the rest of Australia's citizens.[81] *Advance Australia Fair* was declared as our national anthem in 1984, and in this year Western Australia became the last Australian state to abolish capital punishment for murder. The education sector saw the establishment of a Qualifications Framework for Australian universities. *Perfect Match*, a dating show, became hugely popular on national TV, although Philippa Kelly barely noticed this brand new time-waster because her Ph.D. supervisor retired and, finding no one else in her department who specialized in Shakespeare and could take his place, scrapped her Ph.D. thesis on Shakespearean tragedy and began again, eventually submitting three years later without a supervisor.

Such gloomy days of introspection in my own temporarily decentred world were matched by my perception of everything, including the rather slow and inward-looking Nimrod production of *King Lear* staged by Aubrey Mellor at Sydney's Seymour Centre. Mellor was profoundly moved by a century that was edging towards its close after the devastating horrors of two world wars and a holocaust. This provided the thematic basis for his production of *King Lear* – the collapse of the world itself under the pressure of misunderstanding and gross mismanagement. His production opened with a deep red hanging drape that was rent aside by John Bell's Lear to reveal a bare stage littered with the rubble of warfare. Dressed in modern uniforms, Lear's retinue assembled in silence, and several minutes elapsed before any dialogue was spoken. This brought the atmosphere down to a level from which it was difficult to recover, particularly as Bell's whole performance was low-key, in the style of psychological realism. Bell's delivery was designed to highlight the theme of family strife, with an irascible rather than a thunderously regal father, and a movement towards measured disillusionment instead of all-out madness. The understated performance drew quite a lot of criticism from reviewers who had been looking forward to the traditional agony of the role: 'I got no sense of Lear's painful journey out of self-preoccupation. Bell's Lear was never an octogenarian *in extremis*. He remained a rather fit and eccentric 50-year-old.'[82]

Bell himself said in an interview at the time:

I think the play is almost totally pessimistic and is totally atheistic. In fact, I think it mocks conventional religious beliefs of all kinds and the only virtues which exist . . . are endurance, toughness, truth and loyalty.[83]

And, 25 years later in a conversation with me, Bell looked back on the production and remarked, 'If you start with rubble, you don't have anything much to give away. The production didn't really have anywhere to go.'[84] Not even Colin Friels' swaggering performance as a monstrously attractive Edmund could do anything more for the production than ensure that the tittering schoolgirls in the front row were well-seduced.

By the mid-1980s, Australian women had large slices of daily time opened up for them because of certain new conveniences. This was, indeed, what inspired my mother to begin a diary in that year:

Lately the changes taking shape around us seem to be more evident. A baby is now carried in a capsule – a hard plastic-mould outer and soft padded interior, with a safety strap. Milk bottles (600 ml) are being replaced by 2-litre plastic containers, so much easier to store and use and order. And the daily rubbish need no more be incinerated, as the huge new 'wheelie' bins easily take a week's rubbish. The microwave oven has cut cooking back to a minimum, and I'm now needing to have a 3/4 of an hour walk each afternoon to get enough exercise! That I do enjoy.

In 1984 the Country Women's Association was still one of Australia's most active women's groups, with its focus on support for women's morale in the country and its establishment of tea rooms that could make them feel at home when they travelled to the city. Women's rights had not been deeply addressed beyond the establishment of refuges in capital cities. Policies for educating Australian girls for the most part perpetuated conservative attitudes towards women, emphasizing, for example, the 'broadening' of perspectives, the development of 'confidence and self-esteem' in girls, and 'meeting the needs' of girls.[85] Almost fifteen years after the marvellously abrasive debut of Germaine Greer with *The Female Eunuch*, the women's movement in Australia had a certain quietism. *Good-Bye Tarzan: Men After Feminism*',[86] 'Male Feminism',[87] 'Men: Comrades in Struggle',[88] as well as various articles in the 1984 special issue of *Women's Studies International Forum*, were all about how men were coping with women's increased independence.[89]

Sydney-born feminist philosopher Elizabeth Grosz published in that year her first article on a psychoanalytic reading of women's bodies. Today Grosz is a famous and regularly interviewed personage – but back then, her sisters outside (and some inside) the halls of the University of Sydney viewed her kind of thinking as freaky and unrelated to the 'real' world. Perceived contradictions in the behaviour of feminists were seen not in terms of the multivalency they are applauded for today, but as a betrayal that revealed the 'real' lack of commitment in card-carrying feminists. I vividly recall the nose-twitching levelled at Carole Ferrier, an active Queensland advocate for women's rights, simply because she happened to enjoy wearing high-heeled shoes with her jeans.

In this context it is unsurprising that not a lot of complexity was given to the portrayal of the female roles in Mellor's production; and it is quite telling that in recalling the rehearsal process, John Bell has said, 'Well, I wasn't really part of the preparation with the women. Aubrey did that with them on his own.'[90] Regan and Goneril were disappointingly crude, removing items of female clothing to reveal the guerilla uniform of warfare. This effectively endorsed the image Lear offers of women who deny their 'natural' roles by seeking material gain. It is unfortunate that productions that emphasize the female characters' gradual adoption of masculine dress and attributes (evoking the style of Peter Brook's famous 1962 production[91]) align themselves with Lear's curse and undermine the sympathy for the sisters which it requires a special effort of interpretation to achieve.[92] Judy Davis played a coolly contemporary Cordelia, although her doubling performance of the Fool was heart-wrenching.

1998: The Man Who Wasn't There: Kosky's *King Lear*

By the time John Bell again essayed the role of Lear 14 years later, the stability of the early 1980s had been replaced by the challengingly progressive government led by Prime Minister Paul Keating – supporter of the arts, Aboriginal rights and the abolition of the monarchy, and eventually unpopular apologist for 'the recession we had to have' – and, with the access to power by John Howard in 1995, Australia was in a state of flux. 'I love John,' said my mother. 'Not a glamour puss, but a good, good, good, good man.' Not everyone agreed with her as Howard's conservative government made a series of 'adjustments', including the abolition of the Native Title Act. A Goods and Services tax was imposed for the first time in Australian history, and there began a strong movement to trim down the power of unions, whose members were at times portrayed as a bunch of beer-swilling thugs whose buttocks hung lazily out of their pants.

During this time my grandmother became memory-impaired. On her two-month-long visit to my parents' house at the age of 91, she was no longer expected to do the small tasks that had always given her pleasure, stringing beans, shelling prawns or mixing the base for Anzac biscuits. She transformed into a family heirloom sitting gently in the armchair with soft, shell-pink nails expertly manicured by the lady down the street, her scalp translucent now through milky white waves of permed hair. Ever-helpful, Granny still tried, imperfectly, to contribute to the occasion, singing 'La la la la la la la', until my mother said, 'Shut up, Granny.' My mother felt very badly about these occasional moments when she lost her patience – she dearly loved Granny, and I think she saw an awful omen of what she herself might become – but personally I didn't find Granny's singing disturbing, although indeed it was out of tune. It was, for me, a tender reminder that she was still there. And, although she died shortly before Barrie Kosky staged his production of *King Lear* for the Bell Shakespeare Company in 1998, I feel that she had a strangely telepathic relationship to it anyway. Kosky's characters, in their aimlessly chaotic dramatic world, could have sung along with Granny had she still been able to sing.

When asked her opinion of Kosky's production, a student, randomly interviewed by a journalist, said:

and because it's the royal family like, there's perception within the royal family then, people sleeping with people and everything like, it's basically the same now. (Georgia Brown, student)[93]

Had Kosky rehearsed his production in front of students like this one, he might have obtained some useful dramaturgy tips. All that the student could grasp in the production's general mayhem was a parallel with the contemporary antics of the royal family, with its sexual intrigues, reality TV appearances and crazed weight loss activities. There was a royal family of sorts in Kosky's production – an Aboriginal Cordelia (Deborah Mailman) who was the crushed and bloodless victim of her father's egomania, and an androgynous-looking Goneril (Melita Jurisic) and Regan (Di Adams), who spoke in high-pitched whining voices and sucked out Gloucester's eyeballs, eventually murdering Cordelia onstage with a plastic bag. But Lear himself was not really 'there' at the centre of this family. If we think of his character as the pivot of the great wheel that the Fool sees rolling downhill, it did not seem that Lear was 'on' the wheel at all. He had a few great moments, like the bus-station setting I described in Chapter 6. But I didn't get the sense of the dramatic arc he travels in his struggle to understand what happens to him, nor of 'this great decay' that is also his renewal.

The enormous challenge of the old king's experience, as he journeys to the heart of his heath and confronts himself disrobed, was lost in Kosky's production, as John Bell wandered disconsolately around and was directed to hand out plastic dildoes at the door. Parody itself is not antipathetical to Lear's experience – but it has to stand sheer with desperate pain in order to take us inward. Lear, in this production, was flirted with by a singing, tap-dancing female Fool (Louise Fox) who served as his implied fourth 'daughter', memorably singing 'My Heart Belongs to Daddy' (more tunefully than Granny used to sing). With its 1940s Hollywood style, its amalgam of Muscovite cloaks and elaborate head coverings, its servants played as grotesque dogs with huge, flopping penises and its wild, screeching noises, the Kosky production was a Bedlam of sorts. Whole chunks of text were replaced with vaudeville and dance hall routines. Audiences walked out of the production in droves, often shouting, RUBBISH as they left. My feeling was not that it was rubbish, but that it made me strongly aware, in counterpoint, of how this play is perhaps the most internal of all of Shakespeare's tragedies except perhaps for *Macbeth*. If you don't go inward to the heart of *King Lear*, you are left wondering what it is all about, speculating about connections to the madness of the modern royals, or musing, as did critic Fiona Scott-Norman, that after seeing Edgar smearing his excrement over the walls, 'the one thing I can't believe is that I've come out and am eating.'[94]

2010: *King Lear* for a New Millennium

One of the great challenges of *King Lear*, as I mentioned above, is that the process of change in the play is so internal. The play has moments of cataclysmic emotion – the shocking first scene, the eye-gouging – but for much of the action an old man, and his mirror image, try to come to terms with degradation. How does a director make this process dramatic and engaging? This was a question that John Bell and director Marian Potts addressed head-on, and with a striking result, in 2010. Many actors have tried to create and maintain momentum through histrionics. But this is exhausting and, quite quickly, alienating. It is Lear's internal arc that must be journeyed on night after night, so that audiences can believe in it and care about it profoundly. This is an enormous task for an actor.

The 2010 Bell Shakespeare Company production was set on a dais seven paces across which was built onto the stage. In the play's first scene, Bell took Lear from surprise to annoyance to rage, eventually throwing his youngest daughter off the dais so that she lay sprawled and sobbing on the floor, already symbolically cast out of the court. At various points during the performance – as on the heath – the dais would begin revolving. The movement of the dais as the actors walked around it gave the impression of immense distance and exertion. At other points the revolution of the dais could convey the giddiness of a world turned inside out and upside down.

In this production, Bell gave his role the plausibility of the human and the symbolic quality of the more-than-human. Sometimes he was mad, sometimes he was raging, sometimes he was quite rational. You could see him transiting from one emotion, getting stuck in another, transiting back again and forward. These transitions were punctuated by tympani and drums, which sometimes irritatingly drowned out his speeches (and the Fool's), but which also created the essence of pathetic fallacy – the whole world breaking down along with the interior of an old man's mind. Sometimes when Lear was in a rage he would throw something at a big brass disk, creating the real fear in the audience that he could bear no more ('Oh Fool, I shall go mad . . .' [2.2.451]). He was supported by a frail, spare old Fool (Peter Carroll), dressed all in white. As together they endured their ordeal, Lear would go in and out of awareness – sometimes ignoring the Fool, sometimes hearing him and registering his truths, sometimes becoming annoyed with him. The Fool, in this sense, accompanied and articulated Lear's internal arc.

Much attention in this production had been given to the question of how to create interest and complexity for the three daughters. Goneril and Regan were dressed so superbly that you would not have found such figures outside of Government House. Goneril, played by Jane Montgomery, was much taller than her two younger sisters. She was thin, very white, and, right from the beginning, haughty and remote. Regan's part in the play suggests that she is more manipulative, and, as Leah Purcell played her, this subtlety was brought out. She was more expressive than Cordelia, more dissimulating than Goneril. And Cordelia, played by Susan Prior, was dressed, like the Fool, all in white. She was clear and firm: she did not want to symbolically marry her father, she loved him but not 'like that'. Cordelia's steady refusal in this first scene allowed Bell to escalate the rashness of his character in counterpoint.

Oswald was also interestingly played. By turns obsequious and firm, he played a very 'human' servant who highlighted the deadly risk taken by the Fool and Kent in comparison. Whenever things got rough, Oswald would seamlessly depart – and often when he was onstage his thoughts were unreadable. One got the sense that he knew what was happening, but did not want to show it (in contrast to the Fool, who knows what is happening and sees it as his job to show it).

In 2010 the world has become a zone of connection. Airline prices have fallen 44 per cent since the early 1980s, and a remarkable variety of internet facilities and cellular phone devices permit constant contact and updates in knowledge. A navigation device can even allow your hosts to track your progress on your way to dinner. You can take a photo of a meal and put it on Facebook for an unlimited number of people to see. You can have a pregnancy at age 50 with another woman's eggs; you can drive a car connected to the electric power point in your home, and you can connect with the sun to power your power point. And yet all of this connection means that people (in the Western world, at least, who can afford the concept of personal space) have become experts at 'show' while protecting the being within. Much as we might *connect* with each other, humans in the Western world are increasingly unavailable.

This recent Bell production of *King Lear* was built around the idea that it is, in the end, only relationships that compel people and move them to change. Human beings can be in physical circumstances that change enormously, and yet they will still want to be the same. If a physical comfort is taken away, one might initially ask 'Why?' But one is likely to scrabble around to find something that will replace what has been lost. In *King Lear* this is not possible, because everything – not just Lear's home, not just his knights, but his identity itself – is taken away. He symbolically completes this degradation by removing even his own clothes and entering dressed in weeds. But he would not change even with all of these removals were it not for his changed relationships with those around him. 'Pray you, undo this button' (5.3.284) speaks a thousand words of change: the humility of simply being *human* is something that Lear has had to acknowledge. In the end, for human beings, it is relationships that wound us within, it is relationships that comfort and renew us. And this was the beauty of the 2010 Bell Shakespeare *King Lear*. Many reviewers found it quiet and a little dull; but it dared to take its audiences on a three-hour journey within the old man's mind, adumbrated by a beautifully calibrated Gloucester, who came to 'see' when he was blind. Vulnerable, degraded, by turns remorseful and angry, Lear was ready for the arc of change.

* * *

So much for John Bell and his Lears. But what of the girl of 33 years ago? The girl who, when she first made an appearance with her King, had just grown out of riding around Oakey on her bicycle, sleuthing townspeople in the manner of her admired child detectives from Enid Blyton? The girl who, in graduating to *King Lear*, had encountered a psychological landscape that she would revisit again and again?

She has gone to most places in her life with a feeling of sheer chance, and then quickly come to think either that what transpired was meant to be or, upon occasion, an unfortunate mistake that probably happened because she deserved it after all. That girl was me, is me and will probably always be me unless something very radical happens. I have not been spared my own moments on the wretched heath, and the memories of wounds encountered there can still open and bleed. I married a widower and adopted his son, feeling the sheer joy of making a home and coming home, as well as panic at the thought that either of them could be lost to me through that wanton will of the gods that so bewilders Lear and Gloucester. I write, I teach, I travel to Australia to participate in the government area of scholarship awards and to Saudi Arabia to teach accreditation to university women. I work as a dramaturge for the California Shakespeare Theatre, immersing myself in the details of each play as it comes from the shadows into focus for production.

As I grow older I trust in my brain more and more, but still I don't fully trust in my own judgment. This is the legacy of most people's relationship to life, to wounds and to pleasures too soon snatched away. And it is perhaps the facet of myself at which my husband most marvels – my childish longing for life to stay happily ever after even when I have written so extensively about the fact that it doesn't. It is the very feature of life, perhaps, that keeps me coming back to Lear. *The King and I* was never just about a three-hour play, much less a musical: for me it is a story that goes on.

Notes

Introduction

1. For example, on the influential New South Wales Higher School Certificate syllabus, it reigned as the only mandatory Shakespeare text until 2008.

Chapter 1

2. The dismantling of the policy began under the leadership of Liberal Prime Minister Robert Menzies, whose second term of leadership began in 1949 and ran until his retirement in 1966. The architect of this process under Menzies was Sir Hubert Opperman, Australia's champion Olympic cyclist and Immigration Minister in the Menzies government from December 1963 until December 1966. Opperman facilitated a relaxation of conditions for entry into Australia of people of mixed descent. The year 1964 saw the abolition of the mandatory 15-year waiting period for non-Europeans to bring their relatives into Australia. In 1965 the Labor Party deleted reference to 'White Australia' in its party platform, although much of the policy itself still remained. (Note that Arthur Calwell, Gough Whitlam's deputy during the 1960s, made a famous quip about why Asians shouldn't be let into Australia: 'two Wongs don't make a white.' Nonetheless, it was indeed under Whitlam's leadership that the White Australia Policy came to a formal close in 1973.)
3. Alan R. Hirsch aptly describes nostalgia as 'a yearning to return home to the past – more than this, it is a yearning for an idealized past . . . not a true recreation of the past, but rather a combination of many different memories, all integrated together, and in the process all negative

emotions filtered out.' 'Nostalgia: A Neuropsychiatric Understanding', in *Advances in Consumer Research* Volume 19, eds. John F. Sherry, Jr. and Brian Sternthal (Provo: Association for Consumer Research, 1991), pp. 390–95, p. 390.

4. This term was used by William Zak to connote the way in which Lear has the graces of kingship taken from him in a 'disrobing' of self and dignity that will lead him to face his shame. See William Zak, *Sovereign Shame: A Study of 'King Lear'* (Lewisburg: Bucknell University Press, 1984), p. 13.

5. Thirty-five years later, on 18 May 2010, I heard this comment uncannily echoed almost word for word by an old man, Hank, who was reading the play out loud in a Berkeley Senior Center class (taught by playwright James Keller).

6. In contrast to Lear's voluminous speeches (he has 166 lines in the Folio's first scene alone), Regan has only 182 lines in the entire (Folio) play, Goneril 149, and Cordelia 107.

7. Elizabeth Schafer points out *King Lear's* 'vividly expressed and poetically effective misogyny, much of it voiced by Lear himself'. Noting that Lear's tirade against women is positioned late in the play when sympathy for the elderly king is riding high, she says, 'Negotiating this moment without endorsing . . . Lear's deep-seated loathing of women's sexuality presents a serious challenge.' *MsDirecting Shakespeare* (London: Women's Press, 1998), p. 128.

8. Because none of the programme directors or radio hosts whom Reddy contacted in 1973 would play the song, she sang it on 19 different television stations. Women from all over Australia saw the clip and started phoning local radio stations to request the song, which then entered the charts at number ninety-nine and in nine months went to number one. For almost forty years it has been a motivational song for women all over the world, and, indeed, it was played as recently as the Academy Awards in March 2010.

9. Germaine Greer, *The Female Eunuch* (Boulder: Paladin, 1970).

10. Indeed, it is interesting to note that in her later book, *Daddy, We Hardly Knew You*, Greer sought to free her own mind from an obsession with her father, whose physical and then emotional absence had dominated her life.

11. In 1983, David Plante wrote of Germaine Greer: 'She lived, not in the particular country in which she was bodily, but in the general, problematic world which obsessed her.' Greer said in an interview in the 1970s that in Australia 'there is almost no class more loathed than the class of students, of educated larrikins, and therefore by association their long-haired bearded gurus who are giving them the means for subversion' (http://www.takver.com/history/sydney/greer1972.htm, accessed 25 January 2002). (She also said to me very recently, 'The only reason I go to Queensland is to visit my condominium.' Berkeley Hillside Club, 25 March 2009.)

12. 'The Dismissal: A Brief History'. *The Age*, 11 November 2005 www. theage.com.au.

13. 'Never trust a man who wears a top hat and tails in Australia, in Summer,' commentator Neale Towart has said of John Kerr. *Workers Online*, Issue No. 78, 17 November 2000. http://workers.labor.net. au/78/c_historicalfeature_whitlam.html

14. Australia Day broadcast, 26 January 1976. (For partial transcript see http://www.topologymusic.com/davidson/whitlam.htm)

15. Rudd ordered a vast insulation plan to be put in motion, whereby insulation would be installed in thousands of Australian homes. While this was an inspired idea in terms of the need for insulation in all of these homes and in terms of aiding economic recovery, hundreds of firms sprang up as installation specialists. The improper installation of many systems left four people electrocuted. Prime Minister Rudd's failure to discipline Peter Garrett, Minister for the Environment, over a situation that Garrett had reportedly been warned about repeatedly, infuriated the Australian public.

16. Miranda Devine, the *Sydney Morning Herald*, Monday 28 June.

Chapter 2

17. These descriptions of cadet life are from the stories students told me, and from what I observed, fifteen years ago. I cannot speak for what the conditions of the Academy are like in 2011.

18. *King Lear*, by William Shakespeare, with Introduction, ed. Philippa Kelly (Sydney: Halstead Press, 2002).

19. 3.6, which is a part of the Quarto version and not of the Folio version. (Because it is a very famous scene, I included it in my 'Folio' edition of the play in a distinctly differentiated font.)

20. See *Shakespeare Comes to Broadmoor: The Actors are Come Hither. The Performance of Tragedy in a Secure Psychiatric Hospital*, ed. Murray Cox (London: Jessica Kingsley, 1992).

21. In this process, offenders are faced with their victims in a controlled setting in order to confront offenders with the effects of what they have done.

22. 'Hilary's' name has been changed for reasons of privacy.

23. Hillary was referring to Sydney's Bellevoir Theatre.

24. Hillary C., inmate, Mullawah Maximum Security Prison for Women, Sydney, 1997.

25. Thank you to Chandran Kukathas, London School of Economics, for an exchange of ideas on this subject.

26. This distinction between shame and guilt is made by Norman Bales, and I find its clarity very helpful. (http://www.tcoc.net/sermons/GUILT.pdf, accessed 25 February 2009)

27. Ewan Fernie and William Zak have written of the shame that Lear tries to run away from in the play's very first scene. See William Zak, *Sovereign Shame*, and Ewan Fernie, *Shame in Shakespeare* (New York: Routledge, 2001), pp. 173–207.

28. Whether or not *The Winter's Tale* is a reprise of the theme of shame in *King Lear*, or, indeed, a rehearsal for this theme, is still unclear, since the composition date for *The Winter's Tale* has not been fully agreed on. While some critics date *The Winter's Tale* at 1609 or so – shortly before it was first performed – others date it later, and still others argue that it could have been written as early as 1594.

29. Ewan Fernie has put this very movingly:

Trying to buy love reveals exactly what he is at pains to conceal: shame, the feeling that he cannot win affection and admiration for himself. Such shame has led Lear into the disgraceful shamelessness of bartering for the love of his children . . . (*Shame in Shakespeare*, p. 178)

30. This is one of the tenets of recent psychological theories on mental health, where digging through the psyche to excavate the past has been, in some psychotherapeutic practice, replaced with a search for cogency. A gentle and lucid approach to this theme is given in *Parenting From the Inside Out,* by Daniel J. Siegel and Mary Hartzell (New York: Penguin, 2004). For connections via stories between past, present and future, see p. 48. See also p. 129 for reference to the 'coherence' of the present being 'intruded on' by stories from the past.

Chapter 3

31. *Ethical Leadership*, Address at St. Paul's City Ministry, Adelaide, 4 September, 2003. (See http://www.stpaulsethics.com.au/documents/EthicalLeadership.pdf)

32. Winnifred Nowottny. 'Lear's Questions', *Shakespeare Survey* (1), 1957, pp. 90–97.

33. *New Scientist* Issue 2058 (London: Reed Business Information, 30 November, 1996).

34. *The Castle* was directed by Rob Sitch.

35. Transcript of interview with George Negus, 10 June 2004 (See http://www.abc.net.au/gnt/profiles/Transcripts/s1130025.htm, 10 June 2004)

36. John Lahr, *Dame Edna Everage and the Rise of Western Civilization: Backstage with Barry Humphries* (Berkeley: University of California Press, 2000), p. 105.

37. Many thanks to my good friend R. S. White for leading me to this YouTube segment. http://au.youtube.com/watch?v=TdnAaQ0n5–8

38. The reviewer mentioned his pleasure at the fact that Shakespeare's version had been chosen rather than Mr. Tate's. See *The Monitor*, Qtd Eric Irvin, *Theatre Comes to Australia* (Brisbane: University of Queensland Press, 1971). p. 199.

39. The *Sydney Morning Herald*, 26 January, 1837.

40. This cartoon can be found at the following site: http://www.naa.gov.au/naaresources/federation_album/html/1887b.htm

41. BBC Education internet site. *King Lear:* (Interviewer's name not cited). Information available at http://www.bbc.co.uk/education/bookcase/lear/mitchell.shtml

42. I have in my possession an enormous amount of photocopied material that has appeared in print media about *King Lear* in Australia over the years. Time and again (and particularly when a critic is about to launch into a complaint), a company is described as 'brave' for 'tackling' a play as monumental as *King Lear*. 'Bravely director Aubrey Mellor has attempted' his aim of dealing both with the political and familial dimensions of the play; 'and it very nearly comes off', says Michael Morton-Evans of the Nimrod production in 1984. (1 August *Sydney Morning Herald*, 1984). *King Lear* is 'a challenge' (*The Australian*, 1 August 1984). These are just two examples to hand – but almost every review comments on Shakespeare's literary masterpiece that must be ascended like a mountain.

43. Programme notes for Playbox Theatre, Festival of Perth, 1994, p. 5.

44. The play was dropped from the 2009 syllabus in New South Wales – the most influential state syllabus – and replaced by *Hamlet*.

45. Nicky, student at an exclusive Sydney girls' school, quoted in the *Sydney Morning Herald*, 28 Sept 2004.

46. See the 'Board of Studies' site: http://arc.boardofstudies.nsw.edu.au/standards-packs/SP02_15140/files/samples/q2–10/q2–10_b12_s1.pdf

47. See the 'Board of Studies' site: http://arc.boardofstudies.nsw.edu.au/standards-packs/SP02_15140/files/samples/q2–10/q2–10_b12_s1.pdf

48. Lecture delivered at the University of Adelaide Law dinner, 2 August 2008. 'To Speak What We Feel'. For transcript, see http://www.unisa.edu.au/law/docs/LawStudentsDinner2008.pdf

49. See http://www.abc.net.au/am/content/2008/s2448434.htm

50. see http://www.unisa.edu.au/law/docs/LawStudentsDinner2008.pdf

Chapter 4

51. 'After the White-Out', *Arena Magazine* (Melbourne), No. 73, October–November 2004, p. 38.

52. At this point in our history (1976), refugees were pouring into Darwin from Vietnam, where Australia had been involved in the war since the early 1960s. Now that the allies had failed and the war had ruined and endangered the lives of countless Vietnamese on the losing side, there was a strong feeling in Australia that these people should be allowed

to emigrate to Australia where they might find safety and a livelihood. The Whitlam Labor Government of 1975, however, refused to allow into Australia the Vietnamese who were embassy employees, and other Vietnamese who had been involved with the Australian war effort in Vietnam (Prime Minister Whitlam believed that they had Eastern European conservative roots). Additionally, the Labor Party in Australia saw the influx of boat people as a danger to the rights of workers – jobs would be taken that might legitimately go to Australians – which was the origin of the story of the Vietnamese bringing in 'secret gold bars'. In 1976, following the deposition of Whitlam and the installment of Malcolm Fraser's conservative government, Labour Shadow Immigration Minister Mick Young flew up to Darwin to take a two-week look at these hapless, desperate people. A man of great principle and compassion, Young was horrified by their destitution, and flew back to Canberra to assure its politicians that there were no hidden gold bars. He argued, moreover, that these were human beings whose destiny Australia's armed forces had helped to destroy in their own homeland, and whom we had a moral obligation to assist.

53. http://www.politics.ie/foreign-affairs/127541-australia-halts-sri-lankan-afghan-asylum-claims.html

54. Rupert Goold's *King Lear*, which opened in Liverpool in 2009, was set in the riotous, poverty-stricken England of Thatcher's early years, and began with her victory speech of 1979: 'Where there is discord, may we bring harmony.' And on a different tack, in a 2008 article in *Pittsburgh Live* (21 September), a journalist (who preferred to remain anonymous) lauded Margaret Thatcher and suggested that her daughter Carol was Goneril and Regan-like in claiming that her mother has suffered from dementia since 2000.

55. These famous words are spoken by the character of Jennifer (played by Allie McGraw) in the 1970 movie *Love Story*, directed by Arthur Hiller.

Chapter 5

56. To hear this song, go to http://www.youtube.com/watch?v=VuoUrr9_Y8I
57. http://www.squarewheels.com/scottswriting/roadblocks.html

58. http://www.abc.net.au/rn/encounter/stories/2008/2252159.htm

59. See Ewan Fernie, *Shame in Shakespeare*, p. 191.

60. See http://www.melbourne.anglican.com.au/main.php?pg=news&news_id=9299&s=996

61. John Illingsworth, ed. *A Christmas Card in April: Station Life on the Palmer River in the 1940s and 1950s* (Townsville: James Cook University, 1990).

62. Taped by Michael Rimmer in Mooloolaba, 4 October 1974. Now held on CD ROM at James Cook University library, Townsville.

63. For a wonderful discussion of 'civic nationalism', see 'The Curate's Egg', an essay by scholar (and good friend) Martin Krygier in his collection *Civil Passions* (Melbourne: Schwartz, 2005, pp. 43–55). Krygier also refers in another essay in this collection to White Australia's 'failure of moral imagination' which is at the root of much of our blindness. ('Subjects, Objects and the Colonial Rule of Law', *Civil Passions*, pp. 56–91, p. 90). He has recently elaborated the idea of forefathers, national celebrations and national guilt in an as-yet unpublished paper entitled: 'The Meaning of What We have Done: Humanity, Invisibility and the Law in the European Settlement of Australia'.

64. These, in Jacobean England, were most often men.

Chapter 6

65. *Sydney Morning Herald*, 15 November 2003.

66. David Roffney, Webmediadiary, 19 September 2008 (http://webdiary.com.au/?g=node#comment-84694. Roffney also goes on to quote Lear's 'I shall do such things – what they are I yet not know, but they shall be the terrors of the earth . . .' (2.4.275) to indicate the woeful lack of specificity in the rescue plan.

67. http://candobetter.org/node/1584 5 October, 2009.

68. Len Ainsworth has been laughingly depicted as a contemporary *King Lear*, a title he quite happily accepts. Formerly the head of a gaming company, Ainsworth gave away his assets to his seven sons and two ex-wives when he got cancer, and when he recovered he wanted to take them back again. He proceeded to go into competition against them, and remade a substantial amount of his fortune. Michael Wolff describes Australian newspaper magnate Rupert Murdoch as 'King Lear-like – seem[ing] to be

setting his progeny off for just the sort of dynasty-wrangling he's exploited in so many other companies, including Dow Jones.'
(See http://www.latimes.com/features/books/la-et-rutten3–2008dec03,0, 7497625.story)

69. Australian anthropologist Ted Strehlow has been described as taking 'a descent into Lear-like paranoia and semi-madness' (Stephen Bennetts, *Journal of Australian Studies*, No. 78, 2003). Phil Doyle, in *Workers Online*, (2004) describes the plight of Rugby coaches who don't have the grace to retire before they are sacked: they typically run 'a fearful Lear-like press conference that has all the ghoulish intensity of a slow motion car crash...' (See http://workers.labor.net.au/features/200406/b_sportspage_sacks.html.)

70. John W. Longworth. 'Inter-generational Transfers in the Rural Sector: a Review of Some Problems'. *Australian Journal of Agricultural Economics*, 16 (3), 1972, pp. 169–82.

71. I was astonished and moved by a 2007 *Choice Magazine* survey which found that a great number of their wives will give up almost everything to survive the hard times, but not their last store of self-preservation, *La Prairie* face cream, costing $160 a bottle.

72. John Alden, 'Lear: Problems for the Producer', *Sydney Morning Herald*, 19 November 1959.

73. I was lucky enough to see this scene early in the production's run, because soon afterwards Kosky took the production's John Bell (who played Lear) out to breakfast, and asked him to cancel the bus station scene and to hand out plastic dildoes to the cast instead.

74. David Williamson, *Travelling North* (Sydney: Currency Press, 1979).

75. Thea Astley, *Coda* (New York: Putnams, 1994).

76. Helen Garner, *The Spare Room* (New York: Henry Holt, 2008).

Chapter 7

77. Martha Nussbaum, *Cultivating Humanity*. (Cambridge, MA: Harvard University Press, 1997), pp. 90–91.

78. See Ewan Fernie, *Shame in Shakespeare*, p. 201.

79. http://www.wazmac.com/wazza/news_items/2005/april2005/joh_quotes.html

80. A Shakespeare scholar who chooses to remain anonymous has offered the irresistible description of Hawke as 'a bit of an entrepreneurial dead duck but still kindly regarded since he was a legendary drinker in his time and a 'good bloke'. (Email exchange, 4 November 2009).

81. In theory, Aborigines had the right to vote in the mid nineteenth century, when voting rights were given to all British subjects over the age of 21 (which, since we had declared the land *terra nullius* and therefore included Aborigines as British subjects, meant that they had the right to vote as well). Australian women (who included of course Aboriginal women) got the vote in 1895. But very few Aborigines knew their rights, and it was not until the 1960s that full voting rights were accorded to Aboriginal people. (Not surprisingly, Queensland lagged behind by three years, granting full voting rights in 1965.)

82. *The National Times*, 14 to 21 September 1984.

83. Qtd. Suellen O'Grady, *The Australian,* 1 August 1984.

84. Phone conversation on 1 November 2009.

85. Lyn Yates, 'Feminism and State Policy: Questions for the 1990s', in *Feminism and Social justice in Education: International perspectives*, ed. Madeleine Arnot and Kathleen Weiler. (Oxon: Routledge, 1993), pp. 167–85, p. 174.

86. H. Franks, Allen and Unwin, *Goodbye Tarzan : Men after Feminism* (Helen Franks: London and Sydney, 1984).

87. Stephen Heath, in *The Dalhousie Review*, 64 (2), Summer 1984.

88. bell hooks, Chapter 5 in *Feminist Theory: From Margin to Centre* (Boston: South End Press, 1984).

89. Sue Wise and Liz Stanley, 'Male Sexual Politics and Men's Gender Practice' (pp. 13–17); Clive Pearson, 'Anti-Sexist Men: A Case of Cloak-and-Dagger Chauvinism' (pp.29–32); and John Stoltenberg, 'Refusing to Be a Man' (pp. 33–37). *Women's Studies International Forum*, Issue 7.1, 1984.

90. Phone conversation with John Bell, 1 November 2009.

91. In this production for the Royal Shakespeare Company, Paul Scofield played the role of Lear.

92. For more on this point, see Alexander Leggatt, *King Lear* (Manchester: Manchester University Press, 1991), p. 13.

93. See transcript of *Lateline* television programme. http://www.abc.net.au/lateline/stories/s12376.htm

94. See transcript of *Lateline* television programme. http://www.abc.net.au/lateline/stories/s12376.htm

INDEX